T0003900

THE ESSENTIAL Diabetes Instant Pot® COOKBOOK

Healthy, Foolproof Recipes for Your Electric Pressure Cooker

Coco Morante

Photography by Jennifer Davick

TEN SPEED PRESS
California | New York

TO MY HUSBAND, BRENDAN

I'm so proud of how you tackle the daily challenges of life with type 1 diabetes. Here's to many, many more years of good health and good food.

Contents

Foreword

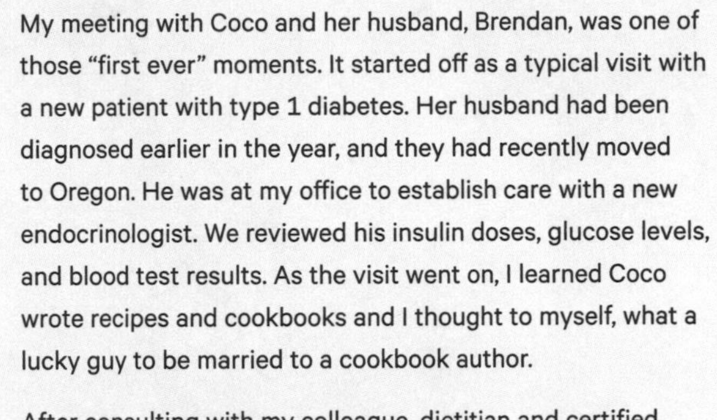

My meeting with Coco and her husband, Brendan, was one of those “first ever” moments. It started off as a typical visit with a new patient with type 1 diabetes. Her husband had been diagnosed earlier in the year, and they had recently moved to Oregon. He was at my office to establish care with a new endocrinologist. We reviewed his insulin doses, glucose levels, and blood test results. As the visit went on, I learned Coco wrote recipes and cookbooks and I thought to myself, what a lucky guy to be married to a cookbook author.

After consulting with my colleague, dietitian and certified diabetes educator Ashley Klees, Coco has created Instant Pot meals that are appealing to and appropriate for those with type 1 diabetes, type 2 diabetes, or prediabetes.

—Jessica Castle, MD

Introduction

When I was in the middle of writing *The Ultimate Instant Pot Cookbook*, something unexpected happened: my husband, who had previously been the picture of perfect health, was diagnosed with type 1 diabetes. I vividly remember the night we figured it out. We had eaten some ribs and mashed potatoes for dinner (made in the Instant Pot, of course), and Brendan was feeling a little bit off afterward. He started making some mental connections; in the previous few weeks he'd been losing weight and experiencing some other unexplained symptoms. A little bit of Googling, a finger prick, and a call to the night nurse confirmed his Dr. Google results, and the next week turned into a blur of appointments and blood tests, followed by a formal diagnosis from an endocrinologist.

The first few weeks were a steep learning curve for both of us. Being the main cook in the house, I was tasked with figuring out the nutrition information (especially carb counts; who knew that "net carbs" equals total carbs minus total fiber?) for all of our meals, while Brendan learned to give himself insulin injections and track his blood sugar with a glucose monitor. We found that his levels were most stable when our meals were low to moderate in carbohydrates, with a good amount of protein and some fat included. After four months of eating this way, his blood work came back with numbers in the range of a person without diabetes.

We now know that diabetes can be managed successfully, and one of the most important pieces of the puzzle is maintaining a nutritious, balanced diet. To that end, preparing your own meals (or in my husband's case, being lucky enough to have a cookbook author prepare them for him) is the most foolproof way to know exactly what's in your food and ensure that you're eating well.

One happy benefit of writing this cookbook has been its usefulness for my own dietary needs, as well as my husband's. With my own diagnosis of polycystic ovary syndrome (PCOS), a condition that's closely tied to insulin resistance, it turns out that the same diet works great for both of us. Though my husband's type 1 diabetes and my PCOS are very different conditions, they can both be managed well with similar foods.

I cannot tell you how excited I was to write this book, not only to help others with diabetes but also to have a resource at home with Instant Pot recipes that my husband and I enjoy. Each recipe includes nutrition information so you don't have to guess at carb counts, and the Instant Pot–specific instructions are clear and easy to follow, telling you which button to press at every step.

Whether you're new to cooking recipes to support diabetes, to using an Instant Pot, or to both, this book is here to guide you on your path to a healthier lifestyle. The introductory pages include all of the beginner Instant Pot information you need, as well as tips on how to eat for type 1 and type 2 diabetes, prediabetes, and other insulin resistance–related conditions.

Oh, and I almost forgot to mention, the food you'll cook will be not only good for you but also delicious and satisfying. Most of the recipes in this book are either hearty one-pot dishes or include simple serving suggestions that make it quick and easy to put together a balanced meal. There are also easy breakfasts, appetizers, and even desserts that you can enjoy without worry.

Wishing you the best of luck on your journey to good health!

Happy (pressure) cooking,
Coco

How to Use the Instant Pot

When you first take your Instant Pot out of the box, do yourself a favor and immediately open the manual and turn to the diagrams. They'll help you get acquainted with the different parts of the Instant Pot, including all of the buttons and light-up indicators on the front and the mechanisms of the lid.

Next, consider joining one or both of these Facebook groups: Instant Pot Community and Instant Pot Recipes. The first is a lively gaggle of participants who will answer your beginner questions in a flash. The second is my page, where I regularly post my own recipes as well as those from my favorite bloggers and cooking websites.

I've tested the recipes in this cookbook in four slightly different 6-quart Instant Pot models: the DUO60, DUO60 Plus, Smart WiFi, and Ultra. These models are my favorites out of the whole Instant Pot line, as they all have a handy notch for resting the lid when the pot is open. They also include a setting for culturing yogurt, which the LUX models do not.

If you are primarily cooking for four people or fewer, I'd go with one of the 6-quart models. If you plan to cook larger pieces of meat (over 4 pounds) or serve a larger crowd on a regular basis, go with the DUO80, DUO80 Plus, or 8-quart Ultra, all of which have an 8-quart capacity. If you are cooking for only one or are extremely short on counter space, opt for one of the 3-quart pots.

No matter which model of Instant Pot you have, the panel on the front has settings for cooking different kinds of foods, adjusting the pot to high or low pressure, regulating the temperature of certain settings, and setting the cooking time. There is also a display that lets you know when the pot is on or off and how much time is left on the program setting once the pot reaches pressure.

You'll select a function key depending on what sort of food is being cooked. In Instant Pot terminology, this translates to pressing a function key to select a cooking program, or selecting a function with the universal dial on the Ultra models. For example, you'll select the Soup/Broth function key to cook a soup, the Rice key to steam a pot of rice, and so on. Each pressure-cooking program can be adjusted to High or Low pressure, as well as Less, Normal, or More cooking time (shown in minutes on the LED display), with Normal being the default setting. You can also adjust the time up or down manually in any setting with the + and - buttons or with the dial, depending on the model.

Instant Pot Settings

Your Instant Pot has multiple cooking programs, or settings, which you'll select based on the type of dish you're preparing. While Instant Pot models vary in which settings are included, they all have a Manual mode, which can be used for most recipes. Here are descriptions of all of the Instant Pot settings.

Bean/Chili

Whether you're cooking a basic pot of beans (see page 152), Indian dal, or chili, use this cooking program. Adjust the cooking time to Less for just-done beans, Normal for soft beans, or More for very soft beans. See the chart on page 158 for exact cooking times for a variety of beans.

Cake

Use the Less, Normal, and More settings according to the recipe you are making, from Fudgy Walnut Brownies (page 138) to New York Cheesecake (page 136).

Egg

You can cook soft-, medium-, or hard-boiled eggs. The Less, Normal, and More settings are timed for extra-large eggs. All of the recipes in this book call for large eggs, so I have decreased the cooking time. You'll need to adjust the cooking times up or down as needed if your eggs are a different size.

Manual/Pressure Cook/Ultra

You can cook any pressure cooker recipe on the Manual setting. Note that this program key is labeled Manual on most Instant Pot models, but some newer models label the same program key as Pressure Cook or Ultra. If you're interested in using recipes written for stove-top pressure cookers, this setting is handy, as those recipes can easily be cooked in the Instant Pot. It opens up a whole world of recipes for you to explore, not just ones meant specifically for the Instant Pot. Stove-top cookers cook faster than the Instant Pot because they operate at slightly higher pressures, so you'll need to increase the cooking time by 15 percent. Depending on the model of Instant Pot you have, you'll use the Adjust or Pressure Level button or the universal dial to toggle between the Low Pressure and High Pressure settings.

Meat/Stew

This one is self-explanatory. Adjust the time to Less, Normal, or More, depending on whether you like your meat cooked soft, very soft, or falling off the bone.

Multigrain

The moderate, even heat of the Multigrain setting is perfect for brown rice and other long-cooking grains. The More setting includes a warm 45-minute presoak before an hour of pressure cooking and is well suited to mixtures of sturdy grains and beans.

Porridge

Use this setting when making rice porridge, oatmeal, or a porridge made of any beans and/or other grains. Always use the natural release method when making porridge, and never fill the pot more than half full to avoid a spattered mess. Cooking porridge under pressure is perfectly safe as long as you stick to those guidelines.

Rice

Any type of white rice can be cooked on this setting. The Less, Normal, and More settings will yield just-tender, tender, and soft rice, respectively. The Ultra models have two automatic Rice programs, for low and high pressure. Using low pressure will yield fluffier rice, while high pressure will yield grains that are softer, with a greater tendency to stick together.

Sauté

The Instant Pot allows you to simmer, sauté, and sear foods before or after cooking them under pressure, a feature that adds to its versatility. This is not a pressure setting, and you should never put the locking lid on when you're using it. You can use a tempered glass lid (see page 11) on this setting to sweat vegetables or to get liquids to reach a boil faster.

The Sauté setting behaves a little differently from the pressure settings, in that it doesn't display a countdown when it's on. While the pot is heating, it will display "On," and it will change to "Hot" once it is fully heated. The default Sauté level is Normal or Medium (it's labeled differently depending on your Instant Pot model), and this is the temperature level used for the recipes in this book, unless indicated otherwise. When I use the Sauté function in a recipe, I usually start cooking right away, without waiting for the pot to preheat. For instance, I put garlic and oil into the pot immediately after selecting Sauté, so the oil heats up at the same time as the pot. This saves a little time.

Instant Pot® Ultra
www.InstantPot.com
Soup/Broth
Meat/Stew
Bean/Chili
Steam
Slow Cook
Sauté
Warm
Rice
Porridge
Multigrain
Cake
Egg
Sterilize
Yogurt
Ultra
Start
Cancel

Additionally, most Instant Pots (with the exception of the LUX models) allow you to adjust the time on the Sauté setting as well as the temperature. If you know exactly how many minutes you'd like to run the Sauté setting (to reduce a sauce or bring a liquid up to a simmer, for instance), you can adjust the time before the cooking program starts. You will not see a countdown on the display, but the pot will turn off once the selected time has passed.

Slow Cook

This function turns your Instant Pot into a slow cooker, with the Less, Normal, and More settings corresponding to the Low, Medium, and High settings on a slow cooker. Because the heating element in the Instant Pot is a focused source in the bottom of the pot, the heat distribution is a little different from that of a slow cooker, however. If you come across a great new slow cooker recipe or have some old favorites that you'd like to make, you can use the Slow Cook setting. When using the Instant Pot for slow cooking (or for any non-pressure setting), a tight seal is not required, so you can use an easy-to-clean tempered glass lid (see page 11), rather than the pressure cooker lid.

Soup/Broth

The heat ramps up a little more gently on this setting than on the Manual setting, which makes it good for simmering soups and broths. Even better, broths turn out clear, not cloudy, when they're cooked under pressure. You'll find recipes for low-sodium roasted beef bone broth, chicken broth, and vegetable broth in the Broths and Pantry Basics chapter.

Steam

The Instant Pot comes with a wire metal steam rack that is used for raising foods off the bottom of the pot when steaming under pressure. You can also use any wire-mesh, silicone, or metal steamer basket. For 3- 6-, and 8-quart Instant Pots, use at least ½, 1, and 1½ cups water, respectively, on the Steam setting. The recipes in this book are written for a 6-quart Instant Pot, so you may need to add more or less liquid for steamed and pot-in-pot recipes (see page 9) if you have a 3- or 8-quart pot.

Sterilize

The Normal setting sterilizes at about 230°F (110°C), and the More setting sterilizes at about 240°F (115°C). This program can be used for baby bottles, canning jars, or any other heat-proof items you want to sterilize.

Yogurt

This setting has two yogurt-related functions: it sterilizes milk on the More or High setting and then turns the milk into yogurt on the Normal or Medium setting. Homemade yogurt is easy to make and more economical than store-bought. You can even culture the yogurt right in a glass container inside the pot using my method on page 28. This is my preferred way to make yogurt, since the ingredients go from Instant Pot to fridge with zero cleanup. The Normal setting is also ideal for proofing bread doughs and batters. The LUX models do not have a yogurt setting.

Operation Keys

These are the buttons that adjust the pressure, cooking time, and, in certain cases, the heat level of whatever cooking program you've selected. Most Instant Pot models have an Adjust button that toggles among the Less, Normal, and More time and heat settings. For pressure settings, it adjusts the time, and for non-pressure settings, including Yogurt, Slow Cook, and Sauté, it adjusts the heat level. The + and - buttons adjust the cooking time up and down, respectively.

The DUO60 Plus has a dedicated Pressure Level button instead of Adjust and/or Pressure buttons, and you press the appropriate function key more than once to toggle among the Less, Normal, and More time and heat settings. The LUX60 model pressure-cooks at only high pressure. It does not have a low pressure setting.

The Ultra has a universal dial that allows you to toggle among all of the cooking programs, pressure settings, heat levels, and cooking times on the Instant Pot, including a highly customizable Ultra setting.

Delay Start

Many Instant Pot models allow you to delay the start of the cooking time for a recipe. You won't find lots of uses for this function, as you typically won't want to leave perishable foods in the Instant Pot for any length of time before cooking them. The one task I do like this function for is soaking and cooking beans and whole grains. I'll often put beans, water, and salt in the pot in the afternoon or evening, delay the time for 8 to 12 hours, and then wake up to perfectly cooked beans in the morning.

Mode and Function Indicators

These are the lights that turn on to indicate what mode (low or high pressure) or function (aka cooking program) is currently selected on the Instant Pot. On models with a keypad interface, all of the function keys and mode indicators have a little white circle that lights up when they are selected. On models with a dial, the selected function is backlit.

Keep Warm/Cancel

This multipurpose button has two separate functions: it cancels any cooking program, and it puts the pot on the Keep Warm setting, similar to the warming setting on a slow cooker. The DUO60, DUO60 Plus, and Ultra models have separate buttons for the Keep Warm and Cancel functions.

The Lid and Releasing Pressure

Now that you know the basic terminology for everything on the front panel of the pot, let's talk about the lid. The lids of the various Instant Pot models (LUX, DUO, Ultra, and SMART) all look slightly different, but they have similar mechanisms. The MAX has a wider range of pressure release modes, including an intermediate setting that allows for a gradual pressure release.

Pressure/Steam Release

The Pressure Release, also called Steam Release on some models, can be set to two positions, Sealing or Venting. When the pot is closed and the Pressure Release is set to Sealing, the pot can come up to pressure. When the cooking program is finished, you can move the Pressure Release to Venting to release the steam from the pot, making it safe to open. And it's okay if the Pressure Release jiggles a bit or seems as if it is not fully secured. It's supposed to feel that way. You can remove it for cleaning as well.

Pressure Releases: Quick, Natural, and Timed Natural

You can release the pressure on the Instant Pot in three different ways.

1. **QUICK PRESSURE RELEASE (QPR)** The moment the cooking program finishes, move the Pressure Release to Venting. This will cause a forceful plume of steam to issue forth, releasing the pressure from the Instant Pot. On the LUX, DUO, Ultra, and Smart WiFi models, you'll manually move the Pressure Release valve to the side, taking care to keep your fingers away from the hot steam. On the Ultra model, the lid has an extra safety mechanism: the Pressure Release button and valve are separate, ensuring your hand is nowhere near the steam. To be extra safe with any model of Instant Pot, use heat-resistant mitts when performing a quick pressure release.

Use the quick pressure release method for the following:

Steamed Vegetables Always release the pressure quickly (immediately after the cooking program ends) when cooking asparagus, broccoli, cauliflower, and any other vegetables you prefer lightly steamed or braised. I'll often set the cooking time to 0 (zero) minutes for these foods, which means they cook only for the time it takes for the pot to come up to pressure plus the time required for a quick pressure release. It's my favorite trick for asparagus, in particular, as it is so easy to overcook it on the stove top.

Soft- or Hard-Boiled Eggs The "set it and forget it" Instant Pot method for boiling eggs means you don't have to wait for and watch a pot of water as it heats on the stove top. A quick pressure release allows you to stop the cooking the moment the cooking program ends, so the yolks never end up with a grayish ring, the telltale sign of overcooked eggs.

Meals in Minutes If you are cooking a recipe with minimal liquid (1 cup or less), so the food won't create foam as it cooks, and the pot is less than half full, you can safely use the quick pressure release method before opening the pot immediately after the cooking program ends.

2. **NATURAL PRESSURE RELEASE (NPR)** Rather than moving the Pressure Release, do nothing. Once a cooking program finishes, the pot will gradually lose pressure on its own as it cools. This can take anywhere from a few minutes to 30 minutes or more. That's because the pot retains more or less heat and pressure depending on the volume of food inside. The pot automatically defaults to its Keep Warm setting at the end of a cooking program, and you can leave it for up to 10 hours before it will shut off completely.

Use the natural pressure release method for the following:

Full Pots of Food If you've filled the Instant Pot to its maximum capacity (half or two-thirds full, depending on the type of food you're cooking), the safest way to open the pot after cooking is with a natural pressure release. This prevents messes that can result from food or liquid sputtering out of the pressure release valve.

Foamy Foods Beans, porridge, and cooked fruits such as applesauce, jams, and compotes have a tendency to sputter and spit if a quick release is used. That's because they typically foam up when boiled or otherwise expand when cooked. Although quick release can work with very small batches of these foods, it is generally safest to let the pressure release naturally, using a timed natural pressure release of at least 10 minutes.

Slow Cooker–Style Convenience The convenience of the Instant Pot lies not only in its ability to cook foods fast but also to hold them at temperature on the Keep Warm setting for up to 10 hours, much like a slow cooker. This means you can put the ingredients in the pot in the morning and set the cooking program. When the cooking is complete, the program will automatically switch to the Keep Warm setting, the pressure will release naturally, and you can come home to a piping-hot meal. Braises, roasts, soups, chilis, and stews hold up particularly well when left on the Keep Warm setting.

Egg Dishes and Cheesecakes Using a timed natural pressure release of at least 10 minutes allows fluffy egg dishes and cheesecakes to settle. In contrast, releasing the pressure quickly can cause these delicate foods to break apart and may make a mess inside the pot.

Delicate Fish Fillets After experimenting with many methods for cooking fish, I've determined my favorite: poach at low pressure and use a natural pressure release. This allows the fish to cook not just while it's under pressure but also from the residual heat on the Keep Warm setting as the pot cools down. Fish comes out evenly cooked and tender, not rubbery or tough, as it often does when the pressure is released quickly.

3. **TIMED NATURAL PRESSURE RELEASE** I often wait 10 or 15 minutes after the end of a cooking program, then move the Pressure Release to Venting to release a less geyser-like amount of steam from the pot.

The pressure release (PR) is given as QPR or NPR for each recipe in this book. When a recipe requires a timed natural pressure release, it's given as a timed NPR (for example, 10 minutes NPR). This means you'll let the pressure release naturally for the listed number of minutes before moving the Pressure Release to its Venting position. If a recipe notes that you should let the pressure release for "at least" a given number of minutes, you may leave the pot to release pressure naturally and stay on its default Keep Warm setting for up to 10 hours.

Use the timed natural release method for the following:

Pasta If you're cooking 1 pound or less of dried pasta (or 8 ounces or less in a 3-quart Instant Pot), the best way to get an al dente result is to set the cooking time for half the time recommended on the package, then let the pressure release naturally for 5 minutes before moving the Pressure Release to Venting and releasing the remaining pressure.

Half-Full Pots The time needed for the initial natural release will vary depending on the volume of food in the pot. It's difficult to come up with a hard-and-fast rule for how long you should wait before Venting. In recipes where I've stated that you should let the pressure release for "at least" a given amount of time, that means you should wait that long after the cooking program ends before manually venting (a timed natural pressure release), or you can leave the pot to release fully naturally. The amount of time required for a timed natural pressure release varies based not only on the volume of the food in the pot but also whether or not it's a food that has a tendency to foam, and whether you're trying to make use of the carryover heat, as in poached fish and seafood recipes.

If you're cooking a half batch of a recipe that would otherwise require a very long natural release, or if the pot is not filled to capacity, the pot will cool down and lose pressure much faster, and it will be safe to open in far less time than a very full pot. As long as you wait the minimum amount of time, you can open the pot whenever it is convenient. If you've doubled the recipe, though, it is safest to let the pressure release fully naturally.

Maximum Fill Levels

No matter what type of pressure cooker you are using, overfilling the pot can result in safety and performance issues, as food can end up clogging the valve and pressure release mechanisms in the lid.

Depending on what you are cooking, you can safely fill your Instant Pot half or two-thirds full. The inner pot in most models is stamped with half and two-thirds fill lines, so make sure the food doesn't come up past the line.

Fill the pot no more than half full for dried beans, grains, pastas, porridges, fruit sauces, and any other foods that can foam up when boiled or that expand when cooked.

Fill the pot no more than two-thirds full for stocks, broths, soups, stews, meaty main dishes, and steamed vegetables.

Pot-in-Pot Cooking and Steam Racks

You may have heard the term *pot-in-pot cooking* from Instant Pot aficionados. It's also sometimes referred to as PIP cooking. This simply means using an additional piece of cookware—cake pan, soufflé dish, Pyrex container, stacked stainless-steel pans (similar to an Indian tiffin carrier)—and nesting it inside the inner pot of the Instant Pot.

This method greatly expands the categories of food you can make in a pressure cooker. Foods that would otherwise scorch on the pot bottom because they include dairy, baked goods such as quiches and cheesecakes, and foods with too little liquid to get up to pressure can be prepared this way. With pot-in-pot cooking, the food is cooked by steam. You put a cup or two of water in the inner pot and the vessel containing the food sits on top of a steam rack.

In this book, I refer to three different kinds of steam racks: wire metal steam rack, tall steam rack, and long-handled silicone steam rack. See the section on Tools and Accessories at right for more information on each of these racks.

Preparation and Cooking Times

You'll notice that each recipe includes a chart with the time required for preparation, cooking, and pressure release. The preparation time, or Prep, starts from the beginning of the recipe instructions and assumes that all of the ingredients are ready to go as described in the ingredient list. The cooking time, or Cook, starts when you turn on the Instant Pot, including any time spent sautéing, the time the pot takes to come up to pressure, and the time the food cooks under pressure. These times are estimates, meant to give you a rough idea of how long it will take to cook a recipe from start to finish—each home cook is different, of course, and variables such as the temperature of ingredients can affect the overall cooking time. If preparation is occurring while the Instant Pot is running a cooking program (if you're assembling a vinaigrette while vegetables steam, for example), that preparation time is not added to the overall time.

Tools and Accessories

You can absolutely start cooking in the Instant Pot without buying additional tools or accessories. If you're like me, though, you'll have fun outfitting your kitchen with a few extras that make Instant Pot cooking even more convenient and enjoyable. Some of these items will expand your recipe repertoire, allowing you to make many dishes that couldn't otherwise be prepared in a pressure cooker, such as New York Cheesecake (page 136). Most of the items listed here are available at any well-stocked cookware store or can be purchased online.

Anti-Block Shield

The little metal cap that fits on the inner part of the exhaust valve on the underside of the lid is the anti-block shield. It helps to keep foamy foods from blocking the valve. It's good practice to remove it and clean it after each use of the pot.

Bowls, Dishes, and Pans

You'll find available a wide variety of bowls, dishes, and pans that fit into the 6-quart Instant Pot for pot-in-pot cooking. My favorites are the Vollrath-brand 1½-quart stainless-steel bowl (both the thinner and thicker ones work well), the Pyrex-brand 7-cup round tempered glass food storage dish, and the stackable stainless-steel pans from Ekovana. I use a 7-inch round springform or removable-bottom cake pan for cheesecakes (these range from 2½ to 3 inches tall) and a 7 by 3-inch round cake pan for cakes, breads, and meat loaf. A 7-inch Bundt pan is also useful for cake making, with pretty, entertaining-friendly results. Ramekins with a 4-ounce (½-cup) capacity are ideal for coddling eggs or making individual omelets.

Extra Inner Pot

If you plan on cooking two Instant Pot dishes in one night or covering the pot and storing it in the fridge, it's nice to have an extra inner pot ready to go. When storing the Instant Pot, I always make sure to leave the inner pot in the housing, in case anyone adds food or liquid to the pot without first checking if the inner pot is in place.

Extra Sealing Rings

The only part of the lid that you'll likely have to replace eventually is the silicone sealing ring, which is seated in a rack inside the perimeter of the lid. It has a life of 6 to 18 months, depending on how frequently you use your Instant Pot. The sealing ring needs to be seated properly in the lid for the pot to come up to pressure, so make sure to replace it securely in the sealing ring rack after you've cleaned it. I keep separate sealing rings for sweet and savory foods because the ring can retain strong odors. Using the Instant Pot–brand blue- and red-colored rings helps me remember which one to use for which purpose.

Fat Separator

Tough cuts of meat well suited for pressure cooking often render a significant amount of fat, and a fat separator is an effective tool for defatting cooking liquids and broths. My preferred models are from OXO. They make both a traditional fat separator with a pouring spout and, my new favorite, an ingenious spring-loaded version with a bottom spout.

Flexible Turner

A flexible turner is ideal for getting under meat patties, chicken pieces, and other foods that can stick when seared in the pot. I'm once again partial to the OXO models, both in heat-resistant nylon and stainless steel.

Immersion Blender

An immersion blender makes quick, low-mess work of blending sauces and gravies, pureeing fruits and vegetables, and emulsifying salad dressings and aioli. It's an indispensable tool in my kitchen, and it's much easier to clean than a countertop blender. Just remember safety first: be sure to unplug the blender and eject the blade assembly from the motor before cleaning.

Kitchen Thermometers

An instant-read thermometer is handy for checking the temperature of meat or poultry to ensure it is cooked through. A probe thermometer with a remote display is useful when making yogurt, as you can set it to beep when it's time to add the culture to the cooled milk.

Kitchen Tongs

Since everything in this book cooks in a deep pot, tongs are for turning and tossing ingredients. The Instant Pot–brand 12-inch tongs are made of sturdy metal and have a solid, well-made spring.

Long-Handled Silicone Steam Rack

This is great for recipes requiring a cake pan or round tempered glass dish. I like the silicone steam rack from Instant Pot and the silicone pressure-cooker sling made by OXO. Both have handles long enough that you can easily lower and lift a pan or dish into and out of the pot, and they are easy to grip.

If you don't have a long-handled silicone steam rack, you can make a sling out of aluminum foil and use it to lower and lift the dish or pan into and out of the pot. To make an **aluminum foil sling**, fold a 20-inch-long sheet of aluminum foil in half lengthwise, then in half again, creating a 3-inch-wide strip. Center it underneath the pan, dish, or other cooking vessel. Pour as much water as the recipe indicates into the Instant Pot and place the wire metal steam rack inside. Firmly grasp the ends of the foil strip and use the strip as a sling to lower the cooking vessel into the pot, on top of the rack. Fold the ends of the sling so they fit into the pot. After cooking, use the sling to lift the cooking vessel out of the pot.

Sautéing Spatula

A wooden or other stiff, heat-safe spatula is what I use when sautéing vegetables or other foods in the Instant Pot. Its slim profile also makes it great for scraping down the sides of the pot, pushing noodles underneath the cooking liquid, nudging browned bits off the bottom of the pan, and stirring up a large amount of food without anything sloshing out of the pot.

Silicone Baking Cups and Mini Loaf Pans

These small-capacity pans are great for cooking individual egg muffins and for freezing foods, including leftovers, in small portions. For muffin-shaped egg bites, I use the Instant Pot–brand 7-inch round silicone egg-bite molds or individual OXO-brand silicone baking cups. Each baking cup has a 2-ounce capacity, and you can fit up to seven cups on the steam rack at one time.

Freezing such staples as broths and sauces in small portions makes for easy meal preparation, as they're quick to thaw, plus you can thaw only the quantity you need. For freezing foods in up to ¾-cup portions, I portion the food into silicone loaf pans, such as the Freshware-brand 6-cavity silicone mini loaf pans, which have a total capacity of 4½ cups. Freeze the food until solid, then unmold, transfer to ziplock plastic freezer bags, label the bags with the date and contents, and store the bags in the freezer.

Silicone Mini Mitts

Any time I refer to "heat-resistant mitts" in this book, I mean a pair of Instant Pot–brand silicone mini mitts. They protect your hands from steam when you vent the lid, and the thin, flexible silicone allows you to grip bowls, pans, and steam racks easily, so you can safely lift them out of the pot.

Spiralizer

A tabletop or handheld vegetable spiralizer is the best and fastest way to make zucchini and sweet potato noodles. Serve vegetable noodles with any dish that calls for pasta for a low-calorie, gluten-free option.

Steamer Basket

A wire-mesh, silicone, or expandable metal steamer basket is necessary for steaming vegetables in the Instant Pot. My favorite Instant Pot–brand models are made of wire-mesh and have easy-to-grasp, solidly attached handles. The fine mesh also makes this the most versatile type of steamer basket, as you can use it for steeping whole spices in drinks such as Masala Chai (page 143).

Tall Steam Rack

This rack allows you to cook two things at once. I often use it to hold a bowl of rice and water above a meat or bean dish cooking directly in the inner pot. (I use a 1½-quart stainless-steel bowl with sloped sides to ensure the rice is submerged fully in liquid. This way, the rice always cooks evenly, even an amount as small as ½ cup.) It's a great hack for cooking other grains, too.

Many different companies make a tall steam rack. Just make sure to purchase one that's 2¾ to 3 inches tall, as it must stand high enough to ensure sufficient clearance between the food in the inner pot and the steam rack.

Tempered Glass Lid

You can purchase a glass lid from Instant Pot, or you can use one from another pot in your kitchen, as long as it fits fairly snugly. I use a glass lid most often on the Sauté setting, usually to bring liquid to a boil quickly or to sweat vegetables. It is also useful for the Slow Cook setting.

Wire Metal Steam Rack

This is the wire metal accessory that comes with your Instant Pot. In the manual, it is referred to simply as the "steam rack." It has arms that can be used to lift foods in and out of the pot. You can use the rack to steam vegetables and eggs as well as ribs, whole chickens, and large roasts that would otherwise be difficult to lift out of the pot. Make sure to wear heat-resistant mitts when touching the rack, as it will be hot when you open the pot.

The Diabetes Pressure-Cooker Pantry

Pressure cooking is done in a hermetically sealed environment. A fair amount of liquid is needed for the pot to seal and come up to pressure, and very little moisture evaporates as the food cooks. This means that flavors don't concentrate in the same way as they would in a Dutch oven on the stove top. To compensate for this, I keep a few go-to ingredients in my pantry to amp up flavor and absorb moisture. Here are my favorites.

Broth Concentrates, Bone Broth, and Bouillon These are incredibly convenient ways to add flavor. When I don't have homemade broth on hand, I like to use the reduced-sodium broth concentrates from Better Than Bouillon and Savory Choice, bone broth concentrates from Kitchen Accomplice, and the vegetarian bouillon cubes from Edward & Sons. I'll often use a blender to combine broth concentrates and bouillon cubes with water quickly, even though the label recommends reconstituting them in boiling water before use.

Curry Paste and Other Spice Pastes and Blends Thai red, green, and massaman curry pastes; Korean gochujang; Moroccan harissa—spice pastes are used in many different cuisines, and they add instant flavor. Thai curry paste makes yellow curry (see page 65) a weeknight-friendly dinner, and harissa adds a sweet and savory aroma to Moroccan-spiced meatballs (see page 49).

Natural and Noncaloric Sweeteners Use these in moderation when sweetening drinks and desserts. As far as natural sweeteners go, agave nectar and brown rice syrup have the more neutral flavor, while coconut nectar has a toasted coconut flavor and the flavor of honey varies depending on the variety. These sweeteners' "natural" designation makes them sound healthful, but in large amounts they will cause blood sugar to spike just as cane sugar or corn syrup do.

Noncaloric sweeteners, on the other hand, do not affect blood sugar levels. Of the ones on the market, Lakanto Monkfruit Sweetener in Classic and Golden varieties give results closest to white and brown sugar, respectively. Both varieties are blends of monk fruit extract and non-GMO erythritol.

Nutritional Yeast If you have a dairy intolerance (or cook for others who do), rest assured you'll find lots of options in this book, a handful of which include savory, cheesy-tasting nutritional yeast. It's my go-to secret ingredient for making dairy-free foods taste like their dairy-based counterparts. In addition to being quite tasty, it contains B vitamins that can be tricky to find in other plant-based foods. Use it in Artichoke Spinach Dip (page 38), No-Bake Spaghetti Squash Casserole (page 96), and Cashew Ranch Dip (page 151).

Oils and Fats Minimal processing is the key to high-quality, health-friendly cooking fats. When purchasing olive oil, look for extra-virgin oil with a production date printed somewhere on the label. For recipes that require a neutral oil, cold-pressed avocado oil or grapeseed oil is ideal. I'll also use butter or coconut oil in moderate amounts when their taste and mouthfeel are preferable to oil. Coconut oil is especially high in saturated fat, so it is best to use it sparingly, in the amount of 1 teaspoon or less per serving. For recipes that require high-heat searing, an oil or cooking fat with a high smoke point, such as avocado oil or ghee, works best.

Shirataki and Vegetable "Noodles" Found in the refrigerated section of grocery stores and natural foods stores, *shirataki* are noodles made from an extremely low-calorie, high-fiber Japanese yam. I like shirataki made by House Foods, which blends yam flour and tofu flour and has a slightly more noodle-like flavor and texture than all-yam shirataki.

For another nutritious, lower-calorie alternative to pasta, use a spiralizer to transform zucchini and sweet potatoes into long strands. Zucchini noodles can be eaten raw or cooked, while sweet potato noodles benefit from a quick sauté. For an even easier option, look for already-spiralized vegetables in the produce section of the grocery store.

Spice and Herb Blends These blends are great for perking up pressure-cooked dishes. I use all types in my cooking, from common ones such as chili powder and Old Bay to herbes de Provence, North African ras el hanout and harissa spice blends, Jamaican jerk seasoning, and Middle Eastern za'atar. I love shopping for these blends at natural foods stores that sell them in bulk. That way, I can buy only as much as I need. When I want to splurge on truly exceptional spice blends, I purchase them from Spice Hound at farmers' markets in the San Francisco Bay Area; Oaktown Spice Shop in Oakland, California; World Spice Merchants in Seattle, Washington; and Penzeys Spices, which has locations throughout the United States. All of these merchants also sell their spices online.

Tamari and Coconut Aminos These are gluten-free alternatives to soy sauce. Tamari is made from soybeans and tends to have a strong flavor, while coconut aminos is made from coconut sap and has a mellower taste. Whichever you choose, read the label carefully before using to make sure it's gluten-free.

Tomato Paste This concentrated form of tomatoes adds body and depth of flavor to tomato-based dishes, so if you're using tomatoes (fresh or canned), double up on the flavor by adding 1 tablespoon of tomato paste as well. Because it can be difficult to get through a can of tomato paste before it goes bad, I buy it in a tube (it keeps a bit longer), or I freeze my canned tomato paste in 1-tablespoon dollops and thaw it as needed.

Vegan Buttery Spread Earth Balance makes a variety of spreads and baking sticks designed to replace butter and shortening. Its Original Buttery Spread can be used in place of butter in nearly any recipe. Just keep in mind that it does contain a bit of salt, so you may want to adjust any other salt in the recipe accordingly.

Worcestershire Sauce and Other Strongly Flavored Condiments These are great when you need an umami flavor bomb to enhance a recipe. They'll improve chilis, stews, and braised meat dishes, making them extra savory. Dijon mustard is a go-to flavor enhancer for me, along with soy sauce, tamari, coconut aminos, fish sauce, miso paste, Sriracha, and sambal oelek. If you keep a gluten-free or vegan diet, look for a brand of Worcestershire that meets your needs. Annie's and Portland brands make vegan varieties (Portland brand is also gluten-free), and the Worcestershire sauces from Edward & Sons Wizard's brand and Whole Foods 365 Everyday Value do not contain gluten ingredients (though the Whole Foods brand sauce is processed in a factory with wheat and other allergens).

Diabetes Nutrition

Many volumes have been written on nutrition for people with diabetes, and the advice can vary based on which type of diabetes—type 1, type 2, or gestational—you are treating. Some basics of diabetes nutrition will benefit just about everyone, however, when it comes to putting together balanced meals that will help keep blood sugar levels steady throughout the day, with fewer highs and lows.

Set a Carbohydrate Goal per Meal

Carbohydrates are the main culprit in causing blood sugar to rise and fall, and so they tend to be the focus of most diabetes-specific nutrition advice. Depending on your gender and activity level, you'll be able to meet your energy needs with a specific amount of carbohydrates per meal (assuming you eat three balanced meals a day). The Harold Schnitzer Diabetes Health Center at Oregon Health & Science University recommends the following amounts of carbohydrates per meal.

Gender	To Lose Weight	To Maintain Weight	For the Very Active
Women	30 to 45 grams	45 to 60 grams	60 to 75 grams
Men	45 to 60 grams	60 to 75 grams	60 to 90 grams

Everyone is a little different, and your mileage may vary when following these guidelines, but they're a great place to start when figuring out what works best for your body.

Tracking your fasting and post-meal blood glucose levels is the best way to determine whether your dietary choices are treating your body well or not. As someone with an insulin resistance–related condition (PCOS) and a family history of type 2 diabetes, I find that erring on the lower carbohydrate end of these ranges works best for me. My husband, who has type 1 diabetes, also finds that his blood glucose levels are at their most stable when he eats a low to moderate amount of carbohydrates. Keeping track of your data will quickly help you to learn your individual tolerance.

Eat Balanced Meals with Carbohydrates, Protein, and Fat

The amount of carbohydrates in a meal is just one facet of diabetes nutrition. Another important piece is keeping things in balance. Meals of carbohydrates alone tend to cause a spike and crash in blood sugar, while meals including all three macronutrients (carbohydrates, protein, and fat) as well as some fiber tend to keep blood sugar more stable.

The Plate Method One easy way to visualize a well-balanced meal is to think of a normal-size dinner plate that is divided in half. Half of the plate is filled with nonstarchy vegetables, the other half is divided evenly between servings of protein and carbohydrate-rich foods. A serving of fat is distributed throughout the entire plate. Whether you're eating at a buffet or putting together a one-pot meal at home, hitting these ratios will automatically get you to a balanced meal. Of course, you can tweak these ratios to suit what works best for you, having more carbohydrates on very active days and less if you're trying to lose weight.

The Hand Method There's another useful visual method that's not only personalized but also goes with you wherever you go: your hand. When putting together a meal, a portion of protein is about the size of your palm, a portion of carbohydrates is about the size of your cupped hand, a clenched fist equals a portion of nonstarchy vegetables, and your thumb is equivalent to a portion of fat. On one end of the spectrum, a woman trying to lose weight might stick to one portion from each category, while on the other end, a very active man might require two portions of each category.

Diabetes in the Real World

The recipes in this book are designed to have a balance of carbohydrates, protein, and fat. If you cook with recipes that are written with your nutritional needs in mind, you won't have to think as much about balancing the macronutrients in your meals. When you want to branch out, or when you're not able to prepare your own food at home, familiarizing yourself with what foods are in each category will help you to make good choices most of the time. One concise list is the American Diabetes Association's "What Can I Eat?" information sheet, which is available online at Diabetes.org. I keep this list on my fridge to inspire grocery shopping trips and to remind me of foods to reach for when I'm out and about.

More Resources Online and Offline

If you want to learn more, check out the American Diabetes Association (ADA) website at Diabetes.org. The ADA website not only offers a wealth of information about food, fitness, and other diabetes basics but can also direct you to diabetes education programs local to your area. Local to me in Portland (and included in the ADA database) is the Harold Schnitzer Diabetes Health Center at Oregon Health & Science University, where my husband sees his doctor and dietitian and where I have taken an excellent one-day course on nutrition for diabetes. Chances are a local hospital or health organization with classes and educational materials is located near you, too.

COOKING ICONS		
	(V) Vegan	(GF) Gluten-Free
	(VG) Vegetarian	(DF) Dairy-Free

1

Breakfast and Brunch

Egg Bites with Sausage and Peppers

SERVES 7 **PREP** 5 minutes **COOK** 15 minutes **PR** 5 minutes NPR **COOL** 5 minutes

Here is a convenient on-the-go breakfast, a packable midmorning snack, or a sit-down meal with some dressed greens or whole-grain toast on the side. These high-protein, low-carb bites are filled with an omelet-inspired mix of turkey sausage, peppers, and onions, then topped with sharp Cheddar cheese.

per egg bite

112 calories

8 grams fat

3 grams carbohydrates

0 gram fiber

8 grams protein

4 large eggs

¼ cup vegan cream cheese (such as Tofutti brand) or cream cheese

¼ teaspoon fine sea salt

¼ teaspoon freshly ground black pepper

3 ounces lean turkey sausage, cooked and crumbled, or 1 vegetarian sausage (such as Beyond Meat brand), cooked and diced

½ red bell pepper, seeded and chopped

2 green onions, white and green parts, minced, plus more for garnish (optional)

¼ cup vegan cheese shreds or shredded sharp Cheddar cheese

In a blender, combine the eggs, cream cheese, salt, and pepper. Blend on medium speed for about 20 seconds, just until combined. Add the sausage, bell pepper, and green onions and pulse for 1 second once or twice. You want to mix in the solid ingredients without grinding them up very much.

Pour 1 cup water into the Instant Pot. Generously grease a 7-cup egg-bite mold or seven 2-ounce silicone baking cups with butter or coconut oil, making sure to coat each cup well. Place the prepared mold or cups on a long-handled silicone steam rack. (If you don't have the long-handled rack, use the wire metal steam rack and a homemade sling as described on page 10.)

Pour ¼ cup of the egg mixture into each prepared mold or cup. Holding the handles of the steam rack, carefully lower the egg bites into the pot.

Secure the lid and set the Pressure Release to **Sealing**. Select the **Steam** setting and set the cooking time for 8 minutes at low pressure. (The pot will take about 5 minutes to come up to pressure before the cooking program begins.)

When the cooking program ends, let the pressure release naturally for 5 minutes, then move the Pressure Release to **Venting** to release any remaining steam. Open the pot. The egg muffins will have puffed up quite a bit during cooking, but they will deflate and settle as they cool. Wearing heat-resistant mitts, grasp the handles of the steam rack and carefully lift the egg bites out of the pot. Sprinkle the egg bites with the cheese, then let them cool for about 5 minutes, until the cheese has fully melted and you are able to handle the mold or cups comfortably.

Pull the sides of the egg mold or cups away from the egg bites, running a butter knife around the edge of each bite to loosen if necessary. Transfer the egg bites to plates, garnish with more green onions (if desired), and serve warm. To store, let cool to room temperature, transfer to an airtight container, and refrigerate for up to 3 days; reheat gently in the microwave for about 1 minute before serving.

Coddled Huevos Rancheros

SERVES 2 **PREP** 5 minutes **COOK** 10 minutes **PR** 5 minutes NPR

Similar to Mexican huevos rancheros, this fresh, colorful, protein-packed dish takes just 20 minutes to make. Although it has fewer carbs and less fat than its namesake, it still makes a satisfying breakfast or brunch. While the eggs are cooking in ramekins in the Instant Pot, you'll warm some black beans on the stove or in the microwave. I like to cook up salsa and beans ahead of time, portion them into freezer bags and freeze them, and then transfer them to the fridge the night before I want to use them. If you are pressed for time, you can use canned beans and store-bought salsa for an even easier recipe without any advance prep.

per serving
383 calories
16 grams fat
35 grams carbohydrates
8.5 grams fiber
23 grams protein

2 teaspoons unsalted butter

4 large eggs

1 cup drained cooked black beans (see page 152), or two-thirds 15-ounce can black beans, rinsed and drained

Two 7-inch corn or whole-wheat tortillas, warmed

½ cup chunky tomato salsa (such as Pace brand)

2 cups shredded romaine lettuce

1 tablespoon chopped fresh cilantro

2 tablespoons grated Cotija cheese

Pour 1 cup water into the Instant Pot and place a long-handled silicone steam rack into the pot. (If you don't have the long-handled rack, use the wire metal steam rack and a homemade sling as described on page 10.)

Coat each of four 4-ounce ramekins with ½ teaspoon butter. Crack an egg into each ramekin. Place the ramekins on the steam rack in the pot.

Secure the lid and set the Pressure Release to **Sealing**. Select the **Steam** setting and set the cooking time for 3 minutes at low pressure. (The pot will take about 5 minutes to come up to pressure before the cooking program begins.)

While the eggs are cooking, in a small saucepan over low heat, warm the beans for about 5 minutes, stirring occasionally. Cover the saucepan and remove from the heat. (Alternatively, warm the beans in a covered bowl in a microwave for 1 minute. Leave the beans covered until ready to serve.)

When the cooking program ends, let the pressure release naturally for 5 minutes, then move the Pressure Release to **Venting** to release any remaining steam. Open the pot and, wearing heat-resistant mitts, grasp the handles of the steam rack and carefully lift it out of the pot.

Place a warmed tortilla on each plate and spoon ½ cup of the beans onto each tortilla. Run a knife around the inside edge of each ramekin to loosen the egg and unmold two eggs onto the beans on each tortilla. Spoon the salsa over the eggs and top with the lettuce, cilantro, and cheese. Serve right away.

NOTE

The yolks of these eggs are fully cooked through. If you prefer the yolks slightly less solid, perform a quick pressure release rather than letting the pressure release naturally for 5 minutes.

Coddled Eggs and Smoked Salmon Toasts

SERVES 4 **PREP** 5 minutes **COOK** 10 minutes **PR** 5 minutes NPR

This is my deluxe take on eggs and toast, with the delicious additions of smoked salmon and fresh herbs and vegetables, plus a generous schmear of Greek yogurt to tie everything together. The eggs are steamed in ramekins in the Instant Pot for easy, hands-off preparation, and you can prepare the toasts while they cook. Use a hearty Nordic or eastern European–style whole-grain rye bread, such as Danish *rugbrød* or German-style *Fitnessbrot* (aka fitness bread). These types of bread will digest more slowly than white bread, keeping your blood sugar more stable and providing you with sustained energy.

per serving
275 calories
12 grams fat
21 grams carbohydrates
5 grams fiber
21 grams protein

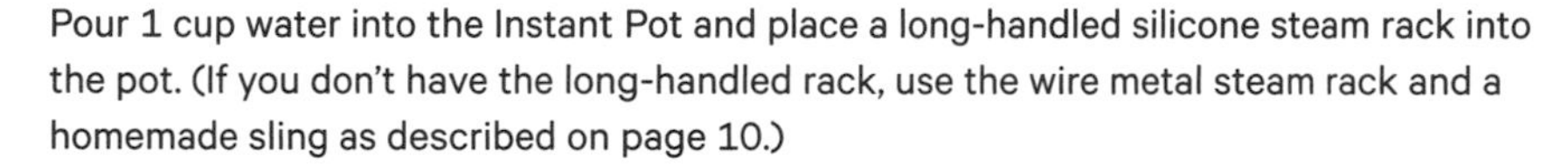

2 teaspoons unsalted butter

4 large eggs

4 slices gluten-free or whole-grain rye bread

½ cup plain 2 percent Greek yogurt (see page 28)

4 ounces cold-smoked salmon, or 1 medium avocado, pitted, peeled, and sliced

2 radishes, thinly sliced

1 Persian cucumber, thinly sliced

1 tablespoon chopped fresh chives

¼ teaspoon freshly ground black pepper

Pour 1 cup water into the Instant Pot and place a long-handled silicone steam rack into the pot. (If you don't have the long-handled rack, use the wire metal steam rack and a homemade sling as described on page 10.)

Coat each of four 4-ounce ramekins with ½ teaspoon butter. Crack an egg into each ramekin. Place the ramekins on the steam rack in the pot.

Secure the lid and set the Pressure Release to **Sealing**. Select the **Steam** setting and set the cooking time for 3 minutes at low pressure. (The pot will take about 5 minutes to come up to pressure before the cooking program begins.)

While eggs are cooking, toast the bread in a toaster until golden brown. Spread the yogurt onto the toasted slices, put the toasts onto plates, and then top each toast with the smoked salmon, radishes, and cucumber.

When the cooking program ends, let the pressure release naturally for 5 minutes, then move the Pressure Release to **Venting** to release any remaining steam. Open the pot and, wearing heat-resistant mitts, grasp the handles of the steam rack and lift it out of the pot.

Run a knife around the inside edge of each ramekin to loosen the egg and unmold one egg onto each toast. Sprinkle the chives and pepper on top and serve right away.

NOTE

The yolks of these eggs are fully cooked through. If you prefer the yolks slightly less solid, perform a quick pressure release rather than letting the pressure release naturally for 5 minutes.

Greek Frittata with Peppers, Kale, and Feta

SERVES 6 **PREP** 5 minutes **COOK** 45 minutes **PR** 10 minutes NPR **COOL** 10 minutes

This frittata is packed with nutritious vegetables, including kale, roasted peppers, and green onions. They are partnered with feta cheese and creamy, thick Greek yogurt, all of which, along with the eggs, help deliver a high-protein, low-carb start to your day. Here the frittata is served with a side of mixed baby greens and tomatoes, but you can also pack just a wedge to eat on the go.

per serving (frittata only)
227 calories
13 grams fat
8 grams carbohydrates
1 gram fiber
18 grams protein

8 large eggs

½ cup plain 2 percent Greek yogurt (see page 28)

Fine sea salt

Freshly ground black pepper

2 cups firmly packed finely shredded kale or baby kale leaves

One 12-ounce jar roasted red peppers, drained and cut into ¼ by 2-inch strips

2 green onions, white and green parts, thinly sliced

1 tablespoon chopped fresh dill

⅓ cup crumbled feta cheese

6 cups loosely packed mixed baby greens

¾ cup cherry or grape tomatoes, halved

2 tablespoons extra-virgin olive oil

Pour 1½ cups water into the Instant Pot. Lightly butter a 7-cup round heatproof glass dish or coat with nonstick cooking spray.

In a bowl, whisk together the eggs, yogurt, ¼ teaspoon salt, and ¼ teaspoon pepper until well blended, then stir in the kale, roasted peppers, green onions, dill, and feta cheese.

Pour the egg mixture into the prepared dish and cover tightly with aluminum foil. Place the dish on a long-handled silicone steam rack, then, holding the handles of the steam rack, lower it into the Instant Pot. (If you don't have the long-handled rack, use the wire metal steam rack and a homemade sling as described on page 10.)

Secure the lid and set the Pressure Release to **Sealing**. Select the **Pressure Cook** or **Manual** setting and set the cooking time for 30 minutes at high pressure. (The pot will take about 15 minutes to come up to pressure before the cooking program begins.)

When the cooking program ends, let the pressure release naturally for 10 minutes, then move the Pressure Release to **Venting** to release any remaining steam. Open the pot and let the frittata sit for a minute or two, until it deflates and settles into its dish. Then, wearing heat-resistant mitts, grasp the handles of the steam rack and lift it out of the pot. Uncover the dish, taking care not to get burned by the steam or to drip condensation onto the frittata. Let the frittata sit for 10 minutes, giving it time to reabsorb any liquid and set up.

In a medium bowl, toss together the mixed greens, tomatoes, and olive oil. Taste and adjust the seasoning with salt and pepper, if needed.

Cut the frittata into six wedges and serve warm, with the salad alongside.

Grain-Free Apple Cinnamon Cake

SERVES 8 **PREP** 10 minutes **COOK** 50 minutes **PR** 10 minutes NPR **COOL** 20 minutes

Best served warm, this sweet and dense cake is scented with cinnamon and studded with chunks of apple—just right for a fall morning. I think of it as more of a breakfast bar than a cake; however, almond flour and Greek yogurt make each slice rich in protein, and the monk fruit–based sweetener keeps it very low in carbohydrates for a stable blood-sugar start to your morning. Leftovers will keep in an airtight container in the fridge for up to 3 days, or they can be cut into wedges, wrapped individually, and frozen for up to 2 months. Pop a wedge into the microwave for a few seconds to warm before serving.

per serving
219 calories
16 grams fat
20 grams carbohydrates
16 grams fiber
9 grams protein

- 2 cups almond flour
- ½ cup Lakanto Monkfruit Sweetener Golden
- 1½ teaspoons ground cinnamon
- 1 teaspoon baking powder
- ½ teaspoon fine sea salt
- ½ cup plain 2 percent Greek yogurt (see page 28)
- 2 large eggs
- ½ teaspoon pure vanilla extract
- 1 small apple, chopped into small pieces

Pour 1 cup water into the Instant Pot. Line the base of a 7 by 3-inch round cake pan with parchment paper. Butter the sides of the pan and the parchment or coat with nonstick cooking spray.

In a medium bowl, whisk together the almond flour, sweetener, cinnamon, baking powder, and salt. In a smaller bowl, whisk together the yogurt, eggs, and vanilla until no streaks of yolk remain. Add the wet mixture to the dry mixture and stir just until the dry ingredients are evenly moistened, then fold in the apple. The batter will be very thick.

Transfer the batter to the prepared pan and, using a rubber spatula, spread it in an even layer. Cover the pan tightly with aluminum foil. Place the pan on a long-handled silicone steam rack, then, holding the handles of the steam rack, lower it into the Instant Pot. (If you don't have the long-handled rack, use the wire metal steam rack and a homemade sling as described on page 10.)

Secure the lid and set the Pressure Release to **Sealing**. Select the **Cake**, **Pressure Cook**, or **Manual** setting and set the cooking time for 40 minutes at high pressure. (The pot will take about 10 minutes to come up to pressure before the cooking program begins.)

When the cooking program ends, let the pressure release naturally for 10 minutes, then move the Pressure Release to **Venting** to release any remaining steam. Open the pot and, wearing heat-resistant mitts, grasp the handles of the steam rack and lift it out of the pot. Uncover the pan, taking care not to get burned by the steam or to drip condensation onto the cake. Let the cake cool in the pan on a cooling rack for about 5 minutes.

Run a butter knife around the edge of the pan to loosen the cake from the pan sides. Invert the cake onto the rack, lift off the pan, and peel off the parchment. Let cool for 15 minutes, then invert the cake onto a serving plate. Cut into eight wedges and serve.

Carrot Cake Oatmeal

SERVES 6 **PREP** 5 minutes **COOK** 30 minutes **PR** 10 minutes NPR

A hearty bowl of oatmeal will satisfy your morning hunger, especially when it's loaded with extra nutrition from carrots and walnuts. A mashed banana is stirred in for some natural sweetness, and a spicy blend of cinnamon, ginger, and nutmeg makes it taste like you're eating a bowl of carrot cake. Adults and kids both love this spin on a healthful breakfast—even my brother's toddler twins couldn't get enough of it when I made it for them! To keep your bowl free from added sugar, use a sugar-free maple syrup. I've put my current favorite in the Note that follows.

per serving
321 calories
17 grams fat
38 grams carbohydrates
7 grams fiber
8 grams protein

2 tablespoons vegan buttery spread or unsalted butter

1½ cups steel-cut oats (gluten-free, if desired)

4½ cups water

8 ounces carrots, finely grated

2 teaspoons ground cinnamon, plus more for serving

¾ teaspoon ground ginger

½ teaspoon ground nutmeg

½ teaspoon fine sea salt

1 ripe banana, peeled and mashed

¾ cup chopped toasted walnuts

Sugar-free maple-flavored syrup (see Note) for serving (optional)

Select the **Sauté** setting on the Instant Pot and melt the buttery spread. Add the oats and cook, stirring often, for about 5 minutes, until the oats are aromatic and lightly toasted. Stir in the water, carrots, cinnamon, ginger, nutmeg, and salt, using a wooden spoon to nudge any browned bits from the bottom of the pot and making sure all of the oats are submerged in the liquid.

Secure the lid and set the Pressure Release to **Sealing**. Press the **Cancel** button to reset the cooking program, then select the **Porridge**, **Pressure Cook**, or **Manual** setting and set the cooking time for 12 minutes at high pressure. (The pot will take about 10 minutes to come up to pressure before the cooking program begins.)

When the cooking program ends, let the pressure release naturally for at least 10 minutes, then move the Pressure Release to **Venting** to release any remaining steam. Open the pot and stir in the banana and any extra liquid sitting on top of the oatmeal.

Ladle the oatmeal into bowls and sprinkle with the nuts and additional cinnamon. Pass the syrup, if desired, when serving.

NOTE

A few brands of sugar-free, maple-flavored syrups are currently on the market. My favorite is the monk fruit–sweetened ChocZero maple syrup. It's thick and rich, has 1 net carb per serving, and is made without sugar alcohols.

Breakfast Millet with Nuts and Strawberries

SERVES 8 **PREP** 0 minute **COOK** 30 minutes **PR** 10 minutes NPR

Millet, a common ingredient in West African cuisine, is a gluten-free grain rich in fiber and protein as well as vitamins and minerals. It has a nutty, corn-like flavor that's sweet and mild, making it an adult- and kid-friendly option for a breakfast porridge. Serve it topped with chopped nuts and strawberries and you'll get enough fuel to start your day.

per serving
270 calories
13 grams fat
35 grams carbohydrates
6 grams fiber
6 grams protein

2 tablespoons coconut oil or unsalted butter

1½ cups millet

2⅔ cups water

½ teaspoon fine sea salt

1 cup unsweetened almond milk or other nondairy milk

1 cup chopped toasted pecans, almonds, or peanuts

4 cups sliced strawberries

Select the **Sauté** setting on the Instant Pot and melt the oil. Add the millet and cook for 4 minutes, until aromatic. Stir in the water and salt, making sure all of the grains are submerged in the liquid.

Secure the lid and set the Pressure Release to **Sealing**. Press the **Cancel** button to reset the cooking program, then select the **Porridge**, **Pressure Cook**, or **Manual** setting and set the cooking time for 12 minutes at high pressure. (The pot will take about 10 minutes to come up to pressure before the cooking program begins.)

When the cooking program ends, let the pressure release naturally for 10 minutes, then move the Pressure Release to **Venting** to release any remaining steam. Open the pot and use a fork to fluff and stir the millet.

Spoon the millet into bowls and top each serving with 2 tablespoons of the almond milk, then sprinkle with the nuts and top with the strawberries. Serve warm.

Yogurt and Greek Yogurt

MAKES 2 QUARTS **PREP** 5 minutes **COOK** 8 hours 20 minutes **PR** N/A **COOL** 30 minutes

per 1 cup
120 calories
5 grams fat
12 grams carbohydrates
0 gram fiber
8 grams protein

½ gallon 2 percent or whole milk

¼ cup plain yogurt with live active cultures, or two 5-gram envelopes freeze-dried yogurt starter

When making yogurt from dairy milk, I find that the lowest-fat milk that still yields good results is 2 percent, also known as reduced-fat milk. If you want a richer yogurt, use whole milk.

You need only two ingredients to make a batch of yogurt in the Instant Pot. Just be sure your Instant Pot has a Yogurt function before you start and you're good to go. The two ingredients are milk and a starter culture (fresh plain yogurt or freeze-dried starter culture will work). You can culture the yogurt right in the inner pot, but I like to use a glass container or jars that fit inside the inner pot. That way, the yogurt goes straight from the Instant Pot to the refrigerator without any additional cleanup required. This recipe yields 2 quarts, a generous amount, but you can make half as much by halving the ingredients and following the same instructions. Once the yogurt is cultured, it can be enjoyed as is or strained to make Greek yogurt (see facing page).

Pour the milk into the Instant Pot and cover with a tempered glass lid or leave the pot open. Select the **Yogurt** setting and adjust the heat to **More** or **High**. This will heat the milk to 180°F, ensuring that it is free of bacteria that could keep it from culturing safely once the starter culture is added.

When the cooking program ends, remove the inner pot and set it on a trivet on the counter. Leave the milk to cool to 115°F, about 30 minutes. (A probe thermometer with a remote display is ideal for this step because you can leave the thermometer in the milk and set it to alert you when the milk has cooled to the proper temperature. Alternatively, you can test the milk periodically with an instant-read thermometer. If you don't have a thermometer, let the milk cool until lukewarm to the touch.) Add the yogurt to the cooled milk and whisk gently until fully incorporated.

Using a jam funnel, ladle the milk into four 1-pint jars or two 1-quart jars. Rinse out the inner pot, return it to the housing, and place the jars into the pot. Cover the pot with the glass lid and select the **Yogurt** setting, making sure it is adjusted to its **Normal** or **Medium** setting. The yogurt will begin to thicken after about 3 hours, but the flavor will be very mild at this point. For a moderately tart yogurt, let it culture for the full 8 hours of the default **Yogurt** program. (If you like your yogurt somewhat tarter or very tart, adjust the program time to 10 or 12 hours, respectively.)

Open the pot and remove the jars. Cover and refrigerate for 6 hours before serving. The yogurt will keep in the refrigerator for up to 2 weeks.

Greek Yogurt Variation

Place a colander over a bowl. Line the colander with a double layer of cheesecloth, a paper towel, or a clean tea towel. Pour the just-made yogurt into the prepared colander, transfer the bowl to the refrigerator, and allow the yogurt to drain until it reaches the desired thickness. This will take from 2 hours for a lightly drained yogurt to overnight for a very thick, spreadable consistency.

per ½ cup Greek yogurt (drained for 12 hours)
85 calories
2 grams fat
4.5 grams carbohydrates
0 gram fiber
11 grams protein

2

Snacks and Appetizers

Smoky Deviled Eggs

SERVES 6 **PREP** 10 minutes **COOK** 15 minutes **PR** 5 minutes NPR **COOL** 10 minutes

When my husband was first diagnosed with diabetes, we were in major need of some low-carb snacks to fill him up between meals. Deviled eggs became one of our favorites early on, and we still have them all the time, both as an afternoon snack and as an appetizer at get-togethers (the recipe is easily doubled). Smoked paprika gives this version a touch of earthiness, and a little hot sauce adds a kick of spicy heat.

per serving (2 halves)
117 calories
10 grams fat
1 gram carbohydrates
0 gram fiber
6 grams protein

6 large eggs

3 tablespoons mayonnaise

1 teaspoon Dijon mustard

1 teaspoon hot sauce (such as Tabasco or Crystal)

¾ teaspoon smoked paprika (sweet or hot), plus more for serving

1 tablespoon chopped fresh chives

Pour 1 cup water into the Instant Pot and place the wire metal steam rack or an egg rack into the pot. Gently place the eggs on the rack, taking care not to crack the eggs as you add them.

Secure the lid and set the Pressure Release to **Sealing**. Select the **Steam** or **Egg** setting and set the cooking time for 5 minutes at high pressure. (The pot will take about 10 minutes to come up to pressure before the cooking program begins.)

While the eggs are cooking, prepare an ice bath.

When the cooking program ends, let the pressure release naturally for 5 minutes, then move the Pressure Release to **Venting** to release any remaining steam. Open the pot and transfer the eggs to the ice bath to cool for about 10 minutes.

Roll each egg around on the countertop to crack the entire shell and loosen the membrane, then, starting at the pointy end of the egg, peel off the shell. Slice the eggs in half lengthwise and transfer the yolks to a medium bowl. Arrange the egg white halves, hollow-side up, on a work surface.

Using a fork, mash the yolks thoroughly. Add the mayonnaise, mustard, hot sauce, and paprika and stir until the ingredients are evenly combined and the filling is smooth. Spoon or pipe the filling into the egg white halves. (At this point, you can store them in an airtight container in the refrigerator for up to 1 day.)

Sprinkle the deviled eggs with the chives and additional paprika before serving.

NOTES

For even a smokier flavor and a little crunch, top the deviled eggs with crumbled cooked bacon.

For a more traditional deviled egg, replace the hot sauce with white wine vinegar, use prepared yellow mustard instead of Dijon, and use sweet paprika instead of smoked paprika.

Southern Boiled Peanuts

MAKES 8 CUPS **PREP** 5 minutes **COOK** 1 hour 20 minutes **PR** 1 hour NPR **COOL** 1½ hours

per ½ cup
160 calories
11 grams fat
8 grams carbohydrates
4 grams fiber
7 grams protein

A Southern specialty, boiled peanuts are a low-carb, high-fiber, high-protein snack. The peanuts are pressure-cooked in their shells with just water and sea salt, and they emerge tender and well-seasoned all the way through. Shell the peanuts and enjoy them at room temperature or chilled as a refreshing snack in warm weather. You'll need to track down raw (not roasted) jumbo peanuts in the shell for this recipe. If you can't find them in grocery stores, Nuts.com is a great online source.

1 pound raw jumbo peanuts in the shell

3 tablespoons fine sea salt

Remove the inner pot from the Instant Pot and add the peanuts to it. Cover the peanuts with water and use your hands to agitate them, loosening any dirt. Drain the peanuts in a colander, rinse out the pot, and return the peanuts to it. Return the inner pot to the Instant Pot housing.

Add the salt and 9 cups water to the pot and stir to dissolve the salt. Select a salad plate just small enough to fit inside the pot and set it on top of the peanuts to weight them down, submerging them all in the water.

Secure the lid and set the Pressure Release to **Sealing**. Select the **Steam** setting and set the cooking time for 1 hour at low pressure. (The pot will take about 20 minutes to come up to pressure before the cooking program begins.)

When the cooking program ends, let the pressure release naturally (this will take about 1 hour). Open the pot and, wearing heat-resistant mitts, remove the inner pot from the housing. Let the peanuts cool to room temperature in the brine (this will take about 1½ hours).

Serve at room temperature or chilled. Transfer the peanuts with their brine to an airtight container and refrigerate for up to 1 week.

Ground Turkey Lettuce Cups

SERVES 8 **PREP** 5 minutes **COOK** 30 minutes **PR** QPR or NPR

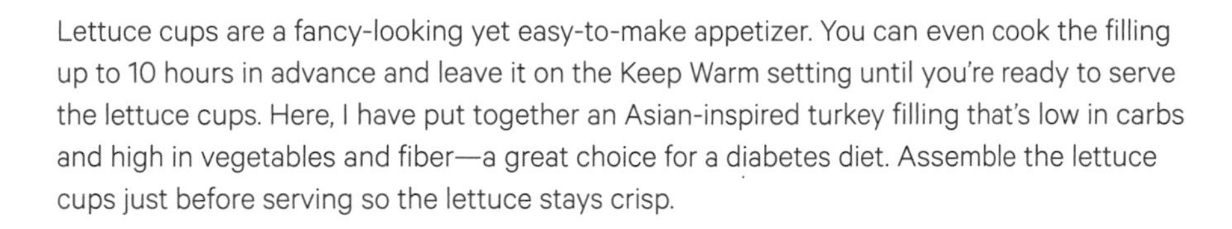

Lettuce cups are a fancy-looking yet easy-to-make appetizer. You can even cook the filling up to 10 hours in advance and leave it on the Keep Warm setting until you're ready to serve the lettuce cups. Here, I have put together an Asian-inspired turkey filling that's low in carbs and high in vegetables and fiber—a great choice for a diabetes diet. Assemble the lettuce cups just before serving so the lettuce stays crisp.

per serving
306 calories
17 grams fat
12 grams carbohydrates
4 grams fiber
26 grams protein

- 3 tablespoons water
- 2 tablespoons soy sauce, tamari, or coconut aminos
- 3 tablespoons fresh lime juice
- 2 teaspoons Sriracha, plus more for serving
- 2 tablespoons cold-pressed avocado oil
- 2 teaspoons toasted sesame oil
- 4 garlic cloves, minced
- 1-inch piece fresh ginger, peeled and minced
- 2 carrots, diced
- 2 celery stalks, diced
- 1 yellow onion, diced
- 2 pounds 93 percent lean ground turkey
- ½ teaspoon fine sea salt
- Two 8-ounce cans sliced water chestnuts, drained and chopped
- 1 tablespoon cornstarch
- 2 hearts romaine lettuce or 2 heads butter lettuce, leaves separated
- ½ cup roasted cashews (whole or halves and pieces), chopped
- 1 cup loosely packed fresh cilantro leaves

In a small bowl, combine the water, soy sauce, 2 tablespoons of the lime juice, and the Sriracha and mix well. Set aside.

Select the **Sauté** setting on the Instant Pot and heat the avocado oil, sesame oil, garlic, and ginger for 2 minutes, until the garlic is bubbling but not browned. Add the carrots, celery, and onion and sauté for about 3 minutes, until the onion begins to soften.

Add the turkey and salt and sauté, using a wooden spoon or spatula to break up the meat as it cooks, for about 5 minutes, until cooked through and no streaks of pink remain. Add the water chestnuts and soy sauce mixture and stir to combine, working quickly so not too much steam escapes.

Secure the lid and set the Pressure Release to **Sealing**. Press the **Cancel** button to reset the cooking program, then select the **Pressure Cook** or **Manual** setting and set the cooking time for 5 minutes at high pressure. (The pot will take about 10 minutes to come up to pressure before the cooking program begins.)

When the cooking program ends, perform a quick pressure release by moving the Pressure Release to **Venting**, or let the pressure release naturally. Open the pot.

In a small bowl, stir together the remaining 1 tablespoon lime juice and the cornstarch, add the mixture to the pot, and stir to combine. Press the **Cancel** button to reset the cooking program, then select the **Sauté** setting. Let the mixture come to a boil and thicken, stirring often, for about 2 minutes, then press the **Cancel** button to turn off the pot.

Spoon the turkey mixture onto the lettuce leaves and sprinkle the cashews and cilantro on top. Serve right away, with additional Sriracha at the table.

NOTE

The turkey mixture can also be treated like a stir-fry and served over cauliflower "rice" or brown rice.

Buffalo Wings with Cashew Ranch Dip

SERVES 8 **PREP** 5 minutes **COOK** 35 minutes **PR** QPR

per serving (wings only)
247 calories
19 grams fat
0 gram carbohydrates
0 gram fiber
19 grams protein

Pressure cooking makes chicken wings incredibly juicy and tender, and a few minutes under the broiler gives them a delicious char. They're a zero-carb snack, making them just the thing to take to a potluck when you want to be sure there will be a snack for you to enjoy. Serve them with my cashew ranch dip, or with a store-bought ranch or blue cheese dressing if dairy works for you. Sprinkle with fresh herbs to add a splash of color.

- 2 pounds chicken wings (drums and flats, tips removed)
- ½ teaspoon garlic powder
- ½ teaspoon sweet paprika
- ½ teaspoon freshly ground black pepper
- 2 tablespoons vegan buttery spread or unsalted butter, melted
- ¼ cup Frank's RedHot sauce
- ½ cup Cashew Ranch Dip (page 151)
- 4 carrots, cut into sticks
- 8 celery stalks, cut into sticks

Sprinkle the chicken wings all over with the garlic powder, paprika, and black pepper.

Pour 1 cup water into the Instant Pot and place the wire metal steam rack into the pot. Place the wings on top of the rack.

Secure the lid and set the Pressure Release to **Sealing**. Select the **Pressure Cook** or **Manual** setting and set the cooking time for 10 minutes at high pressure. (The pot will take about 15 minutes to come up to pressure before the cooking program begins.)

When only a few minutes remain in the cooking program, preheat the broiler. Line a sheet pan with aluminum foil and lightly coat the foil with nonstick cooking spray.

When the cooking program ends, perform a quick release by moving the Pressure Release to **Venting**. Open the pot and, wearing heat-resistant mitts, grasp the handles of the steam rack, lift out the rack with the wings on top, and transfer the wings to a bowl. Add the buttery spread and hot sauce to the bowl and toss to coat the wings evenly.

Using tongs, transfer the wings to the prepared sheet pan. Broil the wings for 5 minutes, flip them over, continue to broil for 4 minutes more, until just beginning to brown and char in spots.

Transfer the wings to a serving platter. Serve warm with the ranch dip, carrots, and celery on the side.

Artichoke Spinach Dip

MAKES 4½ CUPS SERVES 10 **PREP** 0 minute **COOK** 15 minutes **PR** QPR or NPR

A classic party appetizer and a great low-carb option, this tasty dip is packed with nutritious artichokes and spinach, both of which are high in vitamins C and K and folate. Perfect for anyone following a vegan diet, my version is made creamy with cashews instead of the usual dairy. Scoop it up with crudités for a crowd-pleasing snack.

per ¼ cup
127 calories
7 grams fat
10 grams carbohydrates
3.5 grams fiber
6 grams protein

- 1 tablespoon extra-virgin olive oil
- 4 garlic cloves, minced
- 1 large yellow onion, diced
- ½ teaspoon fine sea salt
- ½ teaspoon freshly ground black pepper
- ½ cup low-sodium vegetable broth (see page 150)
- 1½ teaspoons Italian seasoning
- One 12-ounce bag frozen artichoke hearts, thawed according to package directions, drained, and chopped
- One 1-pound bag frozen chopped spinach, thawed according to package directions and squeezed of excess moisture
- 1 cup raw whole cashews, soaked in water to cover for 1 to 2 hours and then drained
- ¼ cup fresh lemon juice
- ¼ cup unsweetened soy milk or almond milk
- 2 tablespoons nutritional yeast

Select the **Sauté** setting on the Instant Pot and heat the oil and garlic for 3 minutes, until the garlic is bubbling but not browned. Add the onion, salt, and pepper and sauté for 4 minutes, until the onion begins to soften. Stir in the broth, Italian seasoning, artichoke hearts, and spinach, using a wooden spoon or spatula to nudge any browned bits from the bottom of the pot and working quickly so not too much liquid evaporates.

Secure the lid and set the Pressure Release to **Sealing**. Press the **Cancel** button to reset the cooking program, then select the **Pressure Cook** or **Manual** setting and set the cooking time for 1 minute at high pressure. (The pot will take about 5 minutes to come up to pressure before the cooking program begins.)

While the vegetables are cooking, in a widemouthed pint jar, combine the cashews, lemon juice, soy milk, and nutritional yeast. Using an immersion blender, blend the mixture for about 2 minutes, until smooth.

When the cooking program ends, perform a quick release by moving the Pressure Release to **Venting**, or let the pressure release naturally. Open the pot and, wearing heat-resistant mitts, lift the inner pot out of the housing. Add the cashew mixture and stir until well combined.

Transfer the dip to a serving bowl and serve warm (see Note).

NOTE

If you're trying to eat fewer simple carbohydrates, forego the usual accompaniments that come with dips, such as baguette slices and potato or tortilla chips, and reach for fresh vegetable crudités instead. Some great options are halved mini bell peppers, cucumbers and large carrots cut on the diagonal, and Belgian endive or Little Gem lettuce leaves.

Green Goddess White Bean Dip

MAKES 3 CUPS SERVES 12 **PREP** 1 minute **COOK** 45 minutes **PR** 15 minutes NPR

Here is a great alternative to hummus, and it's just as easy to make. The beans are cooked in the Instant Pot (no soaking required), then combined with a generous handful of fresh herbs and some lemon juice and extra-virgin olive oil to make a tangy dip with a flavor reminiscent of green goddess dressing. Cut up some vegetables for dipping and you have a nutritious snack. This is also great as part of an appetizer spread for your next party: make Cashew Ranch Dip (page 151), Artichoke Spinach Dip (facing page), and this recipe and serve with a big platter of crudités, wedges of whole-wheat pita, and maybe some tortilla chips.

per ¼ cup
70 calories
5 grams fat
8 grams carbohydrates
4 grams fiber
3 grams protein

1 cup dried navy, great Northern, or cannellini beans

4 cups water

2 teaspoons fine sea salt

3 tablespoons fresh lemon juice

¼ cup extra-virgin olive oil, plus 1 tablespoon

¼ cup firmly packed fresh flat-leaf parsley leaves

1 bunch chives, chopped

Leaves from 2 tarragon sprigs

Freshly ground black pepper

Combine the beans, water, and 1 teaspoon of the salt in the Instant Pot and stir to dissolve the salt.

Secure the lid and set the Pressure Release to **Sealing**. Select the **Bean/Chili**, **Pressure Cook**, or **Manual** setting and set the cooking time for 30 minutes at high pressure if using navy or Great Northern beans or 40 minutes at high pressure if using cannellini beans. (The pot will take about 15 minutes to come up to pressure before the cooking program begins.)

When the cooking program ends, let the pressure release naturally for 15 minutes, then move the Pressure Release to **Venting** to release any remaining steam. Open the pot and scoop out and reserve ½ cup of the cooking liquid. Wearing heat-resistant mitts, lift out the inner pot and drain the beans in a colander.

In a food processor or blender, combine the beans, ½ cup cooking liquid, lemon juice, ¼ cup olive oil, ½ teaspoon parsley, chives, tarragon, remaining 1 teaspoon salt, and ½ teaspoon pepper. Process or blend on medium speed, stopping to scrape down the sides of the container as needed, for about 1 minute, until the mixture is smooth.

Transfer the dip to a serving bowl. Drizzle with the remaining 1 tablespoon olive oil and sprinkle with a few grinds of pepper. The dip will keep in an airtight container in the refrigerator for up to 1 week. Serve at room temperature or chilled.

7-Layer Dip

SERVES 6 **PREP** 10 minutes **COOK** 35 minutes **PR** 20 minutes NPR

A fresh take on a snack-time staple, this colorful, multilayer dip includes more fresh vegetables and less processed ingredients than most versions, with even more vegetables for dipping. It also happens to be dairy-free, gluten-free, and vegan, which makes it ideal for a crowd with a variety of dietary needs. A small batch of black beans are cooked in the Instant Pot using the pot-in-pot technique (see page 9), then seasoned and mashed to make the base of the dip.

per serving (includes chips and vegetables for dipping)

259 calories
8 grams fat
41 grams carbohydrates
8 grams fiber
8 grams protein

CASHEW SOUR CREAM

1 cup raw whole cashews, soaked in water to cover for 1 to 2 hours and then drained
½ cup avocado oil
½ cup water
¼ cup fresh lemon juice
2 tablespoons nutritional yeast
1 teaspoon fine sea salt

BEANS

½ cup dried black beans
2 cups water
½ teaspoon fine sea salt
½ teaspoon chili powder
¼ teaspoon garlic powder

½ cup grape or cherry tomatoes, halved
1 avocado, diced
¼ cup chopped yellow onion
1 jalapeño chile, sliced
2 tablespoons chopped cilantro
6 ounces baked corn tortilla chips
1 English cucumber, sliced
2 carrots, sliced
6 celery stalks, cut into sticks

To make the cashew sour cream: In a blender, combine the cashews, oil, water, lemon juice, nutritional yeast, and salt. Blend on high speed, stopping to scrape down the sides of the container as needed, for about 2 minutes, until very smooth. (The sour cream can be made in advance and stored in an airtight container in the refrigerator for up to 5 days.)

To make the beans: Pour 1 cup water into the Instant Pot. In a 1½-quart stainless-steel bowl, combine the beans, the 2 cups water, and salt and stir to dissolve the salt. Place the bowl on a long-handled silicone steam rack, then, holding the handles of the steam rack, lower it into the Instant Pot. (If you don't have the long-handled rack, use the wire metal steam rack and a homemade sling as described on page 10.)

Secure the lid and set the Pressure Release to **Sealing**. Select the **Bean/Chili**, **Pressure Cook**, or **Manual** setting and set the cooking time for 25 minutes at high pressure. (The pot will take about 10 minutes to come up to pressure before the cooking program begins.)

When the cooking program ends, let the pressure release naturally for at least 20 minutes, then move the Pressure Release to **Venting** to release any remaining steam.

Place a colander over a bowl. Open the pot and, wearing heat-resistant mitts, lift out the inner pot and drain the beans in the colander. Transfer the liquid captured in the bowl to a measuring cup, and pour the beans into the bowl. Add ¼ cup of the cooking liquid to the beans and, using a potato masher or fork, mash the beans to your desired consistency, adding more cooking liquid as needed. Stir in the chili powder and garlic powder.

Using a rubber spatula, spread the black beans in an even layer in a clear-glass serving dish. Spread the cashew sour cream in an even layer on top of the beans. Add layers of the tomatoes, avocado, onion, jalapeño, and cilantro. (At this point, you can cover and refrigerate the assembled dip for up to 1 day.) Serve accompanied with the tortilla chips, cucumber, carrots, and celery on the side.

Hummus with Chickpeas and Tahini Sauce

V   

MAKES 4 CUPS SERVES 16 **PREP** 10 minutes **COOK** 55 minutes **PR** 15 minutes NPR

per ¼ cup (dip only)
107 calories
5.5 grams fat
10.5 grams carbohydrates
4.5 grams fiber
4 grams protein

Topping smooth, creamy hummus with chunky chickpeas is a traditional Middle Eastern serving style. Known in Israel as *hummus masabacha*, the dish delivers the perfect amount of textural contrast. A good addition to a diabetes diet, hummus is high in protein and fiber from the chickpeas and is loaded with good fats from the sesame tahini. Serve with lots of crudités for dipping and scooping.

4 cups water
1 cup dried chickpeas
2½ teaspoons fine sea salt
½ cup tahini
3 tablespoons fresh lemon juice
1 garlic clove
¼ teaspoon ground cumin

Combine the water, chickpeas, and 1 teaspoon of the salt in the Instant Pot and stir to dissolve the salt.

Secure the lid and set the Pressure Release to **Sealing**. Select the **Bean/Chili**, **Pressure Cook**, or **Manual** setting and set the cooking time for 40 minutes at high pressure. (The pot will take about 15 minutes to come up to pressure before the cooking program begins.)

When the cooking program ends, let the pressure release naturally for 15 minutes, then move the Pressure Release to **Venting** to release any remaining steam.

Place a colander over a bowl. Open the pot and, wearing heat-resistant mitts, lift out the inner pot and drain the beans in the colander. Return the chickpeas to the inner pot and place it back in the Instant Pot housing on the **Keep Warm** setting. Reserve the cooking liquid.

In a blender or food processor, combine 1 cup of the cooking liquid, the tahini, lemon juice, garlic, cumin, and 1 teaspoon salt. Blend or process on high speed, stopping to scrape down the sides of the container as needed, for about 30 seconds, until smooth and a little fluffy. Scoop out and set aside ½ cup of this sauce for the topping.

Set aside ½ cup of the chickpeas for the topping. Add the remaining chickpeas to the tahini sauce in the blender or food processor along with ½ cup of the cooking liquid and the remaining ½ teaspoon salt. Blend or process on high speed, stopping to scrape down the sides of the container as needed, for about 1 minute, until very smooth.

Transfer the hummus to a shallow serving bowl. Spoon the reserved tahini mixture over the top, then sprinkle on the reserved chickpeas. The hummus will keep in an airtight container in the refrigerator for up to 3 days. Serve at room temperature or chilled.

NOTES

For a pretty presentation, drizzle extra-virgin olive oil over the assembled bowl, then sprinkle paprika or za'atar on top. A little chopped fresh flat-leaf parsley is a nice addition, too.

Every hummus recipe has its own proportion of tahini, lemon juice, and garlic. Some cooks add olive oil or even a dollop of yogurt. Some include a pinch of ground cumin, though others don't. Play around with this recipe until it suits your taste. You can even blend in a roasted red pepper for a colorful, smoky variation.

3

Meaty Mains

Salisbury Steaks with Seared Cauliflower

SERVES 4 **PREP** 5 minutes **COOK** 30 minutes **PR** 10 minutes NPR

The sauce—a super-savory mix of mushrooms, tomato paste, and beef broth—is my favorite part of this gluten-free Salisbury steak dinner. The sauce is ladled over the tender beef patties, and al dente florets of skillet-seared cauliflower are served alongside.

per serving
362 calories
21 grams fat
21 grams carbohydrates
6 grams fiber
33 grams protein

SALISBURY STEAKS

1 pound 95 percent lean ground beef

⅓ cup almond flour

1 large egg

½ teaspoon fine sea salt

¼ teaspoon freshly ground black pepper

2 tablespoons cold-pressed avocado oil

1 small yellow onion, sliced

1 garlic clove, chopped

8 ounces cremini or button mushrooms, sliced

½ teaspoon fine sea salt

2 tablespoons tomato paste

1½ teaspoons yellow mustard

1 cup low-sodium roasted beef bone broth (see page 149)

SEARED CAULIFLOWER

1 tablespoon olive oil

1 head cauliflower, cut into bite-size florets

2 tablespoons chopped fresh flat-leaf parsley

¼ teaspoon fine sea salt

2 teaspoons cornstarch

2 teaspoons water

To make the steaks: In a bowl, combine the beef, almond flour, egg, salt, and pepper and mix with your hands until all of the ingredients are evenly distributed. Divide the mixture into four equal portions, then shape each portion into an oval patty about ½ inch thick.

Select the **Sauté** setting on the Instant Pot and heat the oil for 2 minutes. Swirl the oil to coat the bottom of the pot, then add the patties and sear for 3 minutes, until browned on one side. Using a thin, flexible spatula, flip the patties and sear the second side for 2 to 3 minutes, until browned. Transfer the patties to a plate.

Add the onion, garlic, mushrooms, and salt to the pot and sauté for 4 minutes, until the onion is translucent and the mushrooms have begun to give up their liquid. Add the tomato paste, mustard, and broth and stir with a wooden spoon, using it to nudge any browned bits from the bottom of the pot. Return the patties to the pot in a single layer and spoon a bit of the sauce over each one.

Secure the lid and set the Pressure Release to **Sealing**. Press the **Cancel** button to reset the cooking program, then select the **Pressure Cook** or **Manual** setting and set the cooking time for 10 minutes at high pressure. (The pot will take about 5 minutes to come up to pressure before the cooking program begins.)

When the cooking program ends, let the pressure release naturally for at least 10 minutes, then move the Pressure Release to **Venting** to release any remaining steam.

To make the cauliflower: While the pressure is releasing, in a large skillet over medium heat, warm the oil. Add the cauliflower and stir or toss to coat with the oil, then cook, stirring every minute or two, until lightly browned, about 8 minutes. Turn off the heat, sprinkle in the parsley and salt, and stir to combine. Leave in the skillet, uncovered, to keep warm.

Open the pot and, using a slotted spatula, transfer the patties to a serving plate. In a small bowl, stir together the cornstarch and water. Press the **Cancel** button to reset the cooking program, then select the **Sauté** setting. When the sauce comes to a simmer, stir in the cornstarch mixture and let the sauce boil for about 1 minute, until thickened. Press the **Cancel** button to turn off the Instant Pot.

Spoon the sauce over the patties. Serve right away, with the cauliflower.

Ground Beef Tacos

SERVES 6 **PREP** 0 minute **COOK** 25 minutes **PR** QPR or NPR

per serving (2 tacos)

353 calories

13 grams fat

28 grams carbohydrates

6 grams fiber

28 grams protein

This taco recipe is fast and flexible: you'll make a well-seasoned ground beef mixture in the Instant Pot, then serve it right away or leave it on the Keep Warm setting for up to 10 hours. A serving of two tacos has a moderate amount of carbohydrates, lots of protein, and a good dose of fiber, so your blood sugar won't spike as it would with a rice-stuffed burrito or a full-on taco plate with starchy sides. The meat is so flavorful that you won't miss the traditional cheese topping, replaced here with dairy-free vegetables and tangy hot sauce.

FILLING

1 tablespoon cold-pressed avocado oil or other neutral oil

2 garlic cloves, minced

1 yellow onion, diced

1½ pounds 95 percent lean ground beef

2 tablespoons chili powder

½ cup low-sodium roasted beef bone broth (see page 149)

Fine sea salt

1 tablespoon tomato paste

Twelve 7-inch corn tortillas, warmed

1 cup chopped white onion

1 cup chopped tomatoes

2 tablespoons chopped fresh cilantro

1 large avocado, pitted, peeled, and sliced

Hot sauce (such as Cholula or Tapatío) for serving

To make the filling: Select the **Sauté** setting on the Instant Pot and heat the oil and garlic for 2 minutes, until the garlic is bubbling but not browned. Add the yellow onion and sauté for about 3 minutes, until it begins to soften. Add the ground beef and sauté, using a wooden spoon or spatula to break up the meat as it cooks for about 3 minutes more; it's fine if some streaks of pink remain, the beef does not need to be cooked through. Stir in the chili powder, bone broth, and ½ teaspoon salt. Dollop the tomato paste on top. Do not stir it in.

Secure the lid and set the Pressure Release to **Sealing**. Press the **Cancel** button to reset the cooking program, then select the **Pressure Cook** or **Manual** setting and set the cooking time for 10 minutes at high pressure. (The pot will take about 5 minutes to come up to pressure before the cooking program begins.)

When the cooking program ends, you can either perform a quick pressure release by moving the Pressure Release to **Venting**, or you can let the pressure release naturally and leave the pot on the **Keep Warm** setting for up to 10 hours. Open the pot and give the meat a stir. Taste for seasoning and add more salt, if needed.

Using a slotted spoon, spoon the meat onto the tortillas. Top with the white onion, tomatoes, cilantro, and avocado and serve right away. Pass the hot sauce at the table.

Moroccan-Spiced Bulgur Meatballs with Yogurt Sauce

SERVES 8 **SOAK** 30 minutes **PREP** 10 minutes **COOK** 35 minutes **PR** 10 minutes NPR

The secret to these tender meatballs is bulgur wheat. It is made by cracking whole-grain wheat into small pieces and parboiling it, so it cooks much faster than whole wheat berries. (For a gluten-free version of these meatballs, use brown rice; see variation.) Steam a spaghetti squash while the bulgur wheat is soaking, and you'll multitask your way to a meal of North Africa–inspired spiced meatballs and spaghetti squash, all topped with a cooling, herb-flecked yogurt sauce mixed with chopped cucumber. I like Persian cucumbers because you can use the whole thing—skin, seeds, and all.

per serving (2 meatballs with tomato sauce and 2 tablespoons yogurt sauce)

252 calories
6 grams fat
25 grams carbohydrates
4 grams fiber
23 grams protein

MEATBALLS

1 cup coarse-grind bulgur wheat
1 cup boiling water
1½ pounds 95 percent lean ground beef
½ large yellow onion, diced
2 teaspoons harissa spice paste, spice blend, or ras el hanout
1 teaspoon fine sea salt

TOMATO SAUCE

1 tablespoon extra-virgin olive oil
2 garlic cloves, minced
½ large yellow onion, diced
One 15-ounce can tomato sauce
¼ cup chopped fresh cilantro
¾ cup water

To make the meatballs: In a medium heatproof bowl, combine the bulgur and boiling water, cover with a silicone lid or a plate, and let soak for 30 minutes, or until the bulgur is soft and the water is absorbed.

Add the beef, onion, harissa, and salt to the bulgur and, using your hands, mix thoroughly. Using ¼ cup of the mixture for each meatball, roll the mixture between your palms to make a total of sixteen meatballs.

To make the tomato sauce: Select the **Sauté** setting on the Instant Pot and heat the oil and garlic for 2 minutes, until the garlic is bubbling but not browned. Add the onion and sauté for 3 minutes, until it begins to soften. Stir in the tomato sauce, cilantro, and water, using a wooden spoon to nudge any browned bits from the bottom of the pot.

Add the meatballs to the pot in a single layer, using the spoon to nudge them into place and working quickly so not too much liquid evaporates. They should just fit.

Secure the lid and set the Pressure Release to **Sealing**. Press the **Cancel** button to reset the cooking program, then select the **Pressure Cook** or **Manual** setting and set the cooking time for 20 minutes at high pressure. (The pot will take about 10 minutes to come up to pressure before the cooking program begins.)

CONTINUED ›

Moroccan-Spiced Bulgur Meatballs with Yogurt Sauce, continued

YOGURT SAUCE

½ cup plain 2 percent Greek yogurt (see page 28)

1 Persian cucumber, finely diced

2 tablespoons chopped fresh cilantro

1 garlic clove, crushed or grated

¼ teaspoon fine sea salt

Steamed Spaghetti Squash (page 155) for serving

2 tablespoons chopped fresh cilantro

To make the yogurt sauce: While the meatballs are cooking, in a small bowl, stir together the yogurt, cucumber, cilantro, garlic, and sea salt. Set aside.

When the cooking program ends, let the pressure release naturally for at least 10 minutes, then move the Pressure Release to **Venting** to release any remaining steam.

Spoon portions of the spaghetti squash into serving bowls. Open the pot and use a spoon or ladle to transfer the meatballs to the squash, arranging them on top. Spoon some of the tomato sauce over the meatballs, then dollop the yogurt sauce on top, or pass at the table. Sprinkle with the cilantro and serve.

Brown Rice Meatball Variation

To make this recipe gluten-free, substitute short-grain brown rice for the bulgur wheat and boiling water.

Pour water into the Instant Pot (1 cup water for a 3- or 6-quart pot, or 1½ cups water for an 8-quart pot), place a wire metal steam rack into the pot, then place a stainless-steel bowl on top of the steam rack. Add 1 cup short-grain brown rice and 1¼ cups water to the bowl, and give the bowl a shake so the rice and liquid settle in an even layer.

Secure the lid and set the Pressure Release to **Sealing**. Select the **Pressure Cook** or **Manual** setting and set the cooking time for 25 minutes at high pressure. (The pot will take about 10 minutes to come up to pressure before the cooking program begins.)

When the cooking program ends, let the pressure release naturally for 10 minutes, then move the Pressure Release to **Venting** to release any remaining steam. Open the pot and, wearing heat-resistant mitts, lift out the bowl of cooked rice. Remove the steam rack and pour out the water in the inner pot.

Fluff the rice with a fork and let it cool to room temperature (about 20 minutes), then proceed with the recipe.

Carnitas Burrito Bowls

SERVES 6 **PREP** 10 minutes **COOK** 1 hour **PR** 20 minutes NPR

The Instant Pot and a sheet pan are all you'll need for these burrito bowls built of brown rice, black beans, crunchy vegetables, and crispy shredded pork. Even though they're much lower in carbs than tortilla-wrapped burritos, they are still plenty satisfying. The pork cooking liquid doesn't go to waste. You'll use it to cook the rice and warm the beans while the pork crisps in the oven.

per serving
447 calories
20 grams fat
35 grams carbohydrates
9 grams fiber
31 grams protein

CARNITAS

1 tablespoon chili powder

½ teaspoon garlic powder

1 teaspoon ground coriander

1 teaspoon fine sea salt

½ cup water

¼ cup fresh lime juice

One 2-pound boneless pork shoulder butt roast, cut into 2-inch cubes

RICE AND BEANS

1 cup Minute brand brown rice (see Note)

1½ cups drained cooked black beans (see page 152), or one 15-ounce can black beans, rinsed and drained

To make the carnitas: In a small bowl, combine the chili powder, garlic powder, coriander, and salt and mix well.

Pour the water and lime juice into the Instant Pot. Add the pork, arranging the pieces in a single layer. Sprinkle the chili powder mixture evenly over the pork.

Secure the lid and set the Pressure Release to **Sealing**. Select the **Meat/Stew** setting and set the cooking time for 30 minutes at high pressure. (The pot will take about 10 minutes to come up to pressure before the cooking program begins.)

When the cooking program ends, let the pressure release naturally for at least 15 minutes, then move the Pressure Release to **Venting** to release any remaining steam. Open the pot and, using tongs, transfer the pork to a plate or cutting board.

While the pressure is releasing, preheat the oven to 400°F.

Wearing heat-resistant mitts, lift out the inner pot and pour the cooking liquid into a fat separator. Pour the defatted cooking liquid into a liquid measuring cup and discard the fat. (Alternatively, use a ladle or large spoon to skim the fat off the surface of the liquid.) Add water as needed to the cooking liquid to total 1 cup (you may have enough without adding water).

To make the rice and beans: Pour the 1 cup cooking liquid into the Instant Pot and add the rice, making sure it is in an even layer. Place a tall steam rack into the pot. Add the black beans to a 1½-quart stainless-steel bowl and place the bowl on top of the rack. (The bowl should not touch the lid once the pot is closed.)

Secure the lid and set the Pressure Release to **Sealing**. Press the **Cancel** button to reset the cooking program, then select the **Pressure Cook** or **Manual** setting and set the cooking time for 15 minutes at high pressure. (The pot will take about 5 minutes to come to pressure before the cooking program begins.)

While the rice and beans are cooking, using two forks, shred the meat into bite-size pieces. Transfer the pork to a sheet pan, spreading it out in an even layer. Place in the oven for 20 minutes, until crispy and browned.

To make the pico de gallo: While the carnitas, rice, and beans are cooking, in a medium bowl, combine the tomatoes, onion, jalapeño, cilantro, lime juice, and salt and mix well. Set aside.

When the cooking program ends, let the pressure release naturally for 5 minutes, then move the Pressure Release to **Venting** to release any remaining steam. Open the pot and, wearing heat-resistant mitts, remove the bowl of beans and then the steam rack from the pot. Then remove the inner pot. Add the green onions and cilantro to the rice and, using a fork, fluff the rice and mix in the green onions and cilantro.

Divide the rice, beans, carnitas, pico de gallo, lettuce, and avocados evenly among six bowls. Serve warm, with the hot sauce on the side.

NOTES

Because of how it's processed, 1 cup uncooked Minute brand brown rice is lower in carbohydrates than 1 cup uncooked regular long-grain brown rice. If using regular long-grain brown rice, increase the cooking liquid to 1¼ cups, increase the cooking time to 20 minutes, and note that each serving will have about an additional 10 grams of carbohydrates per serving.

I find that Early Girl and Campari tomatoes are especially flavorful, which makes them a good choice for eating raw. Romas, sold in most grocery stores, will work, too.

PICO DE GALLO

8 ounces tomatoes (see Note), diced

½ small yellow onion, diced

1 jalapeño chile, seeded and finely diced

1 tablespoon chopped fresh cilantro

1 teaspoon fresh lime juice

Pinch of fine sea salt

¼ cup sliced green onions, white and green parts

2 tablespoons chopped fresh cilantro

3 hearts romaine lettuce, cut into ¼-inch-wide ribbons

2 large avocados, pitted, peeled, and sliced

Hot sauce (such as Cholula or Tapatío) for serving

Red Wine Pot Roast with Winter Vegetables

SERVES 6 **PREP** 10 minutes **COOK** 1 hour 35 minutes **PR** 15 minutes NPR and QPR

per serving
448 calories
25 grams fat
26 grams carbohydrates
6 grams fiber
26 grams protein

Swap parsnips for the potatoes in traditional pot roast and you'll reduce the carb count while adding sweet, earthy flavor, a big plus for anyone following a diabetes diet. The cooking liquid for the pot roast becomes a savory red wine sauce, spiked with garlic, rosemary, and Dijon mustard. This one-pot meal boasts everything you need for a warming wintertime dinner.

One 3-pound boneless beef chuck roast or bottom round roast (see Note)

2 teaspoons fine sea salt

1 teaspoon freshly ground black pepper

1 tablespoon cold-pressed avocado oil

4 large shallots, quartered

4 garlic cloves, minced

1 cup dry red wine

2 tablespoons Dijon mustard

2 teaspoons chopped fresh rosemary

1 pound parsnips or turnips, cut into ½-inch pieces

1 pound carrots, cut into ½-inch pieces

4 celery stalks, cut into ½-inch pieces

Put the beef onto a plate, pat it dry with paper towels, and then season all over with the salt and pepper.

Select the **Sauté** setting on the Instant Pot and heat the oil for 2 minutes. Using tongs, lower the roast into the pot and sear for about 4 minutes, until browned on the first side. Flip the roast and sear for about 4 minutes more, until browned on the second side. Return the roast to the plate.

Add the shallots to the pot and sauté for about 2 minutes, until they begin to soften. Add the garlic and sauté for about 1 minute more. Stir in the wine, mustard, and rosemary, using a wooden spoon to nudge any browned bits from the bottom of the pot. Return the roast to the pot, then spoon some of the cooking liquid over the top.

Secure the lid and set the Pressure Release to **Sealing**. Press the **Cancel** button to reset the cooking program, then select the **Meat/Stew** setting and set the cooking time for 1 hour 5 minutes at high pressure. (The pot will take about 5 minutes to come up to pressure before the cooking program begins.)

When the cooking program ends, let the pressure release naturally for at least 15 minutes, then move the Pressure Release to **Venting** to release any remaining steam. Open the pot and, using tongs, carefully transfer the pot roast to a cutting board. Tent with aluminum foil to keep warm.

Add the parsnips, carrots, and celery to the pot.

Secure the lid and set the Pressure Release to **Sealing**. Press the **Cancel** button to reset the cooking program, then select the **Pressure Cook** or **Manual** setting and set the cooking time for 3 minutes at low pressure. (The pot will take about 10 minutes to come up to pressure before the cooking program begins.)

When the cooking program ends, perform a quick pressure release by moving the Pressure Release to **Venting**. Open the pot and, using a slotted spoon, transfer the vegetables to a serving dish. Wearing heat-resistant mitts, lift out the inner pot and pour the cooking liquid into a gravy boat or other serving vessel with a spout. (If you like, use a fat separator to remove the fat from the liquid before serving.)

If the roast was tied, snip the string and discard. Carve the roast against the grain into ½-inch-thick slices and arrange them on the dish with the vegetables. Pour some cooking liquid over the roast and serve, passing the remaining cooking liquid on the side.

NOTE

I prefer to use a chuck roast for making a pot roast, but you can also use the leaner and more economical bottom round roast. If using bottom round, carve it a bit thinner for serving—about ¼ inch thick—and, as with the chuck, make sure to slice against the grain.

Pork Chops Pomodoro

SERVES 6 **PREP** 0 minute **COOK** 30 minutes **PR** 10 minutes NPR

This low-calorie, fresh take on pork chops is one of my favorite ways to serve them in summer, when cherry tomatoes and basil are at their peak. I keep the carb count low—and avoid blood-sugar spikes—by accompanying them with spiralized vegetable noodles or cauliflower "rice." If you can afford more carbs in your diet, pair the chops with whole-grain pasta.

per serving
265 calories
13 grams fat
3 grams carbohydrates
1 gram fiber
31 grams protein

- 2 pounds boneless pork loin chops, each about 5⅓ ounces and ½ inch thick
- ¾ teaspoon fine sea salt
- ½ teaspoon freshly ground black pepper
- 2 tablespoons extra-virgin olive oil
- 2 garlic cloves, chopped
- ½ cup low-sodium chicken broth (see page 148) or vegetable broth (see page 150)
- ½ teaspoon Italian seasoning
- 1 tablespoon capers, drained
- 2 cups cherry tomatoes
- 2 tablespoons chopped fresh basil or flat-leaf parsley
- Spiralized zucchini noodles, cooked cauliflower "rice," or cooked whole-grain pasta for serving
- Lemon wedges for serving

Pat the pork chops dry with paper towels, then season them all over with the salt and pepper.

Select the **Sauté** setting on the Instant Pot and heat 1 tablespoon of the oil for 2 minutes. Swirl the oil to coat the bottom of the pot. Using tongs, add half of the pork chops in a single layer and sear for about 3 minutes, until lightly browned on the first side. Flip the chops and sear for about 3 minutes more, until lightly browned on the second side. Transfer the chops to a plate. Repeat with the remaining 1 tablespoon oil and pork chops.

Add the garlic to the pot and sauté for about 1 minute, until bubbling but not browned. Stir in the broth, Italian seasoning, and capers, using a wooden spoon to nudge any browned bits from the bottom of the pot and working quickly so not too much liquid evaporates. Using the tongs, transfer the pork chops to the pot. Add the tomatoes in an even layer on top of the chops.

Secure the lid and set the Pressure Release to **Sealing**. Press the **Cancel** button to reset the cooking program, then select the **Pressure Cook** or **Manual** setting and set the cooking time for 10 minutes at high pressure. (The pot will take about 5 minutes to come up to pressure before the cooking program begins.)

When the cooking program ends, let the pressure release naturally for at least 10 minutes, then move the Pressure Release to **Venting** to release any remaining steam. Open the pot and, using the tongs, transfer the pork chops to a serving dish.

Spoon the tomatoes and some of the cooking liquid on top of the pork chops. Sprinkle with the basil and serve right away, with zucchini noodles and lemon wedges on the side.

NOTE

If you like, once the pork chops are finished cooking, you can warm your zucchini noodles or cauliflower "rice" in the cooking liquid. Transfer the chops and tomatoes to a serving plate and cover with foil to keep warm. Select the **Sauté** setting and cook the zucchini noodles or cauliflower "rice" in the liquid for about 2 minutes, just until cooked through.

Shepherd's Pie with Cauliflower-Carrot Mash

SERVES 6 **PREP** 10 minutes **COOK** 35 minutes **PR** QPR

We eat a lot of mashed cauliflower in my house, so my husband and I were excited to discover that cauliflower is even tastier when mixed with naturally sweet carrots. Plus, the combination has many fewer carbs than mashed potatoes. Here, the mash is spread over a hearty, well-seasoned mixture of ground lamb and beef and baby lima beans. If you prefer, you can use all beef for a leaner, milder-flavored filling. Either way, you'll sit down to a high-protein, satisfying meal.

per serving
437 calories
18 grams fat
33 grams carbohydrates
9 grams fiber
39 grams protein

- 1 tablespoon coconut oil
- 2 garlic cloves, minced
- 1 large yellow onion, diced
- 1 pound ground lamb
- 1 pound 95 percent lean ground beef
- ½ cup low-sodium vegetable broth (see page 150)
- 1 teaspoons dried thyme
- 1 teaspoon dried sage
- 1 teaspoon freshly ground black pepper
- 1¾ teaspoons fine sea salt
- 2 tablespoons Worcestershire sauce
- One 12-ounce bag frozen baby lima beans, green peas, or shelled edamame
- 3 tablespoons tomato paste
- 1 pound cauliflower florets
- 1 pound carrots, halved lengthwise and then crosswise (or quartered if very large)
- ¼ cup coconut milk or other nondairy milk
- ½ cup sliced green onions, white and green parts

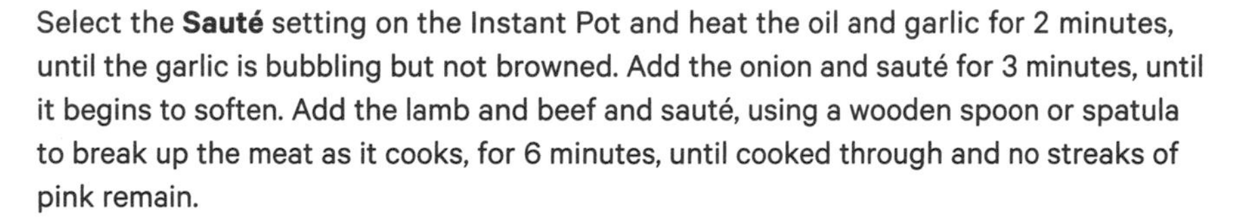

Select the **Sauté** setting on the Instant Pot and heat the oil and garlic for 2 minutes, until the garlic is bubbling but not browned. Add the onion and sauté for 3 minutes, until it begins to soften. Add the lamb and beef and sauté, using a wooden spoon or spatula to break up the meat as it cooks, for 6 minutes, until cooked through and no streaks of pink remain.

Stir in the broth, using the spoon or spatula to nudge any browned bits from the bottom of the pot. Add the thyme, sage, pepper, ¾ teaspoon of the salt, the Worcestershire sauce, and lima beans and stir to mix. Dollop the tomato paste on top. Do not stir it in.

Place a tall steam rack in the pot, then place the cauliflower and carrots on top of the rack.

Secure the lid and set the Pressure Release to **Sealing**. Press the **Cancel** button to reset the cooking program, then select the **Pressure Cook** or **Manual** setting and set the cooking time for 4 minutes at low pressure. (The pot will take about 15 minutes to come up to pressure before the cooking program begins.)

Position an oven rack 4 to 6 inches below the heat source and preheat the broiler.

When the cooking program ends, perform a quick pressure release by moving the Pressure Release to **Venting**. Open the pot and, using tongs, transfer the cauliflower and carrots to a bowl. Add the coconut milk and remaining 1 teaspoon salt to the bowl. Using an immersion blender, blend the vegetables until smooth.

Wearing heat-resistant mitts, remove the steam rack from the pot. Stir ½ cup of the mashed vegetables into the filling mixture in the pot, incorporating the tomato paste at the same time. Remove the inner pot from the housing. Transfer the mixture to a broiler-safe 9 by 13-inch baking dish, spreading it in an even layer. Dollop the mashed vegetables on top and spread them out evenly with a fork. Broil, checking often, for 5 to 8 minutes, until the mashed vegetables are lightly browned.

Spoon the shepherd's pie onto plates, sprinkle with the green onions, and serve hot.

BBQ Ribs and Broccoli Slaw

SERVES 6 **PREP** 10 minutes **COOK** 50 minutes **PR** QPR

On their own, ribs are a great choice for a diabetes-friendly dinner. It's the overly sweet sauces and starchy sides that are commonly served with the ribs that are the carb culprits. I've scanned the grocery aisles to find my favorite barbecue sauces that are also low in sugar (see Note), and I serve my ribs with a generous mound of chopped broccoli slaw instead of potato or macaroni salad. The yogurt-based dressing for the slaw is rich and tangy, and apples add sweetness, so you won't miss the typical sugar-laden dressing.

per serving
392 calories
15 grams fat
19 grams carbohydrates
4 grams fiber
45 grams protein

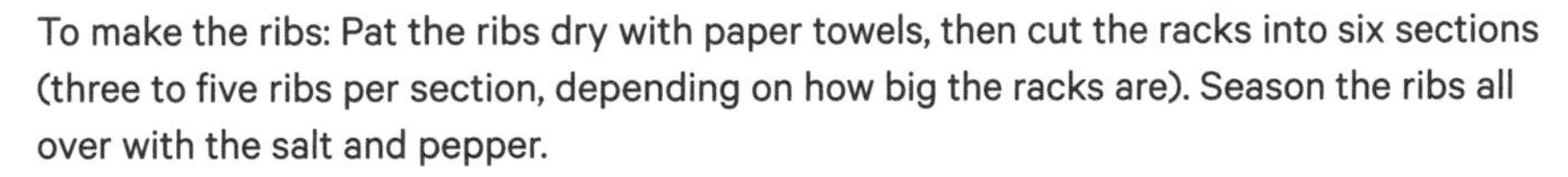

BBQ RIBS

4 pounds baby back ribs

1 teaspoon fine sea salt

1 teaspoon freshly ground black pepper

BROCCOLI SLAW

½ cup plain 2 percent Greek yogurt (see page 28)

1 tablespoon olive oil

1 tablespoon fresh lemon juice

½ teaspoon fine sea salt

¼ teaspoon freshly ground black pepper

1 pound broccoli florets (or florets from 2 large crowns), chopped

10 radishes, halved and thinly sliced

1 red bell pepper, seeded and cut lengthwise into narrow strips

1 large apple (such as Fuji, Jonagold, or Gala), thinly sliced

½ red onion, thinly sliced

¾ cup low-sugar or unsweetened barbecue sauce

To make the ribs: Pat the ribs dry with paper towels, then cut the racks into six sections (three to five ribs per section, depending on how big the racks are). Season the ribs all over with the salt and pepper.

Pour 1 cup water into the Instant Pot and place the wire metal steam rack into the pot. Place the ribs on top of the wire rack (it's fine to stack them up).

Secure the lid and set the Pressure Release to **Sealing**. Select the **Pressure Cook** or **Manual** setting and set the cooking time for 20 minutes at high pressure. (The pot will take about 15 minutes to come up to pressure before the cooking program begins.)

To make the broccoli slaw: While the ribs are cooking, in a small bowl, stir together the yogurt, oil, lemon juice, salt, and pepper, mixing well. In a large bowl, combine the broccoli, radishes, bell pepper, apple, and onion. Drizzle with the yogurt mixture and toss until evenly coated.

When the ribs have about 10 minutes left in their cooking time, preheat the oven to 400°F. Line a sheet pan with aluminum foil.

When the cooking program ends, perform a quick pressure release by moving the Pressure Release to **Venting**. Open the pot and, using tongs, transfer the ribs in a single layer to the prepared sheet pan. Brush the barbecue sauce onto both sides of the ribs, using 2 tablespoons of sauce per section of ribs. Bake, meaty-side up, for 15 to 20 minutes, until lightly browned.

Serve the ribs warm, with the slaw on the side.

NOTE

When buying barbecue sauce, read all of the nutrition labels to seek out the one with the lowest sugar content. Good options are Classic BBQ Sauce from Primal Kitchen, which has no added sugar, and Stubb's (in the Original and Spicy versions), which has just 4 grams sugar per serving.

4

Poultry Mains

Chicken Adobo and Cauliflower Fried "Rice"

SERVES 6 **PREP** 5 minutes **COOK** 30 minutes **PR** 10 minutes NPR

In this version of chicken adobo, a classic dish of the Philippines, authentic flavor is balanced with healthfulness. I use coconut aminos in place of soy sauce, since its mild flavor needs only a touch of brown sugar to create the sweet-and-sour flavor typical of the original. While the chicken finishes cooking, you'll sauté a skillet of cauliflower "rice," a healthful take on *sinangág*, or garlic-fried rice.

per serving
349 calories
12 grams fat
13 grams carbohydrates
3 grams fiber
46 grams protein

CHICKEN

3 pounds bone-in, skin-on chicken thighs

1 yellow onion, sliced

4 garlic cloves, chopped

⅓ cup coconut aminos

3 tablespoons coconut vinegar or rice vinegar

1 tablespoon packed brown sugar

1 teaspoon black peppercorns

3 bay leaves

CAULIFLOWER FRIED "RICE"

1½ tablespoons coconut oil, ghee, or other fat with high smoke point

4 garlic cloves, chopped

1 pound riced cauliflower

¼ teaspoon fine sea salt

2 green onions, white and green parts, sliced

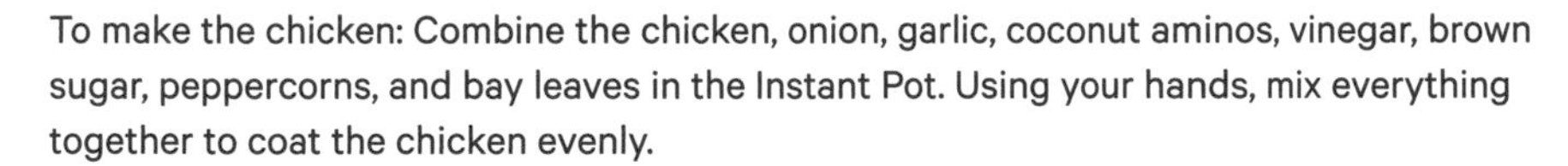

To make the chicken: Combine the chicken, onion, garlic, coconut aminos, vinegar, brown sugar, peppercorns, and bay leaves in the Instant Pot. Using your hands, mix everything together to coat the chicken evenly.

Secure the lid and set the Pressure Release to **Sealing**. Select the **Poultry**, **Pressure Cook**, or **Manual** setting and set the cooking time for 15 minutes at high pressure. (The pot will take about 15 minutes to come up to pressure before the cooking program begins.)

When the cooking program ends, let the pressure release naturally for at least 10 minutes, then move the Pressure Release to **Venting** to release any remaining steam.

To make the cauliflower fried "rice": While the pressure is releasing, in a large skillet over medium heat, warm the oil and garlic together for about 4 minutes, until the garlic is a light toasty brown but not burned. Add the cauliflower and salt and sauté for another 2 to 3 minutes, until the cauliflower is just cooked through. Turn off the heat and stir in the green onions.

Open the pot, transfer the chicken to plates, and spoon the cauliflower "rice" alongside. Ladle some of the cooking liquid over the chicken and serve hot.

Speedy Chicken Cacciatore

SERVES 6 **PREP** 5 minutes **COOK** 30 minutes **PR** QPR or NPR

Boneless, skinless chicken thighs are used for this chicken cacciatore, which means it's lower in saturated fat than most versions and cooks much faster. The flavorful sauce is full of bell peppers, onions, and tomatoes, so there's no need to make a vegetable side dish (though you can certainly serve a green salad if you like). Accompany the chicken with brown rice or whole-grain pasta.

per serving
297 calories
11 grams fat
16 grams carbohydrates
3 grams fiber
32 grams protein

2 pounds boneless, skinless chicken thighs

1½ teaspoons fine sea salt

½ teaspoon freshly ground black pepper

2 tablespoons extra-virgin olive oil

3 garlic cloves, chopped

2 large red bell peppers, seeded and cut into ¼ by 2-inch strips

2 large yellow onions, sliced

½ cup dry red wine

1½ teaspoons Italian seasoning

½ teaspoon red pepper flakes (optional)

One 14½-ounce can diced tomatoes and their liquid

2 tablespoons tomato paste

Cooked brown rice or whole-grain pasta for serving

Season the chicken thighs on both sides with 1 teaspoon of the salt and the black pepper.

Select the **Sauté** setting on the Instant Pot and heat the oil and garlic for 2 minutes, until the garlic is bubbling but not browned. Add the bell peppers, onions, and remaining ½ teaspoon salt and sauté for 3 minutes, until the onions begin to soften. Stir in the wine, Italian seasoning, and pepper flakes (if using). Using tongs, add the chicken to the pot, turning each piece to coat it in the wine and spices and nestling them in a single layer in the liquid. Pour the tomatoes and their liquid on top of the chicken and dollop the tomato paste on top. Do not stir them in.

Secure the lid and set the Pressure Release to **Sealing**. Press the **Cancel** button to reset the cooking program, then select the **Poultry**, **Pressure Cook**, or **Manual** setting and set the cooking time for 12 minutes at high pressure. (The pot will take about 15 minutes to come up to pressure before the cooking program begins.)

When the cooking program ends, perform a quick pressure release by moving the Pressure Release to **Venting**, or let the pressure release naturally. Open the pot and, using tongs, transfer the chicken and vegetables to a serving dish.

Spoon some of the sauce over the chicken and serve hot, with the rice on the side.

NOTE

For a thicker, richer sauce, once you've transferred the chicken and vegetables to a serving dish, cover the dish with foil to keep warm, then select the **Sauté** setting and let the sauce reduce, stirring occasionally, for 15 minutes (it will reduce by about 1 cup). Spoon the thickened sauce over the chicken and serve.

Thai Yellow Curry with Chicken Meatballs

SERVES 4   **PREP** 5 minutes   **COOK** 30 minutes   **PR** QPR or NPR

Chicken meatballs aren't traditional in Thai curries, but they sure are delicious (and economical, too). These are cooked in a spicy sauce that's enriched with coconut milk and loaded with healthful carrots, zucchini, and mushrooms. You can also substitute 1 pound boneless, skinless chicken breast or tenders, cut into bite-size pieces, for the meatballs, if you like. Either way, definitely go to an Asian grocery store to track down a good yellow curry paste, such as one made by Mae Ploy or Aroy-D brand.

per serving
349 calories
15 grams fat
34 grams carbohydrates
5 grams fiber
30 grams protein

1 pound 95 percent lean ground chicken

⅓ cup gluten-free panko (Japanese bread crumbs)

1 egg white

1 tablespoon coconut oil

1 yellow onion, cut into 1-inch pieces

One 14-ounce can light coconut milk

3 tablespoons yellow curry paste

¾ cup water

8 ounces carrots, halved lengthwise, then cut crosswise into 1-inch lengths (or quartered if very large)

8 ounces zucchini, quartered lengthwise, then cut crosswise into 1-inch lengths (or cut into halves, then thirds if large)

8 ounces cremini mushrooms, quartered

Fresh Thai basil leaves for serving (optional)

Fresno or jalapeño chile, thinly sliced, for serving (optional)

1 lime, cut into wedges

Cooked cauliflower "rice" for serving

In a medium bowl, combine the chicken, panko, and egg white and mix until evenly combined. Set aside.

Select the **Sauté** setting on the Instant Pot and heat the oil for 2 minutes. Add the onion and sauté for 5 minutes, until it begins to soften and brown. Add ½ cup of the coconut milk and the curry paste and sauté for 1 minute more, until bubbling and fragrant. Press the **Cancel** button to turn off the pot, then stir in the water.

Using a 1½-tablespoon cookie scoop, shape and drop meatballs into the pot in a single layer.

Secure the lid and set the Pressure Release to **Sealing**. Select the **Pressure Cook** or **Manual** setting and set the cooking time for 5 minutes at high pressure. (The pot will take about 5 minutes to come up to pressure before the cooking program begins.)

When the cooking program ends, perform a quick pressure release by moving the Pressure Release to **Venting**, or let the pressure release naturally. Open the pot and stir in the carrots, zucchini, mushrooms, and remaining 1¼ cups coconut milk.

Press the **Cancel** button to reset the cooking program, then select the **Sauté** setting. Bring the curry to a simmer (this will take about 2 minutes), then let cook, uncovered, for about 8 minutes, until the carrots are fork-tender. Press the **Cancel** button to turn off the pot.

Ladle the curry into bowls. Serve piping hot, topped with basil leaves and chile slices, if desired, and the lime wedges and cauliflower "rice" on the side.

Chicken Shawarma Salad Bowls

SERVES 6 **PREP** 5 minutes **COOK** 35 minutes **PR** QPR or NPR

Here, tender chicken is cooked with a Middle Eastern spice blend, then shredded and piled onto a crisp salad of romaine, cucumbers, peppers, and tomatoes. A garlicky homemade vinaigrette and a dollop of hummus make for a satisfying, flavorful salad. The carb count of this bowl is very low, so you can add a whole-grain flatbread or some pita crackers alongside if your regimen allows. My husband likes a side serving of carbs if he's gone on a run before dinner. On rest days, he sticks with just the salad. Either way, we love sharing this big, easy, high-protein salad on a weeknight.

per serving
364 calories
24 grams fat
15 grams carbohydrates
6 grams fiber
32 grams protein

- 2 teaspoons extra-virgin olive oil
- 2 garlic cloves, minced
- 1 red onion, sliced
- 2 pounds boneless, skinless chicken breasts or thighs
- ½ cup low-sodium chicken broth (see page 148) or water
- 2 tablespoons shawarma seasoning blend (such as Spicely, Pereg, or Sadaf brand)

LEMON VINAIGRETTE

- ⅓ cup extra-virgin olive oil
- ¼ cup fresh lemon juice
- 1 tablespoon red wine vinegar
- 1 tablespoon water
- 1 garlic clove, minced
- ½ teaspoon fine sea salt
- ¼ teaspoon freshly ground black pepper

- 2 tablespoons fresh lemon juice
- 3 hearts romaine lettuce, chopped
- One 6-ounce bag baby spinach
- 1½ cups cherry tomatoes, halved
- 1 English cucumber, sliced
- 1 large red bell pepper, seeded and thinly sliced
- 1½ cups hummus (see page 42)
- 3 tablespoons chopped fresh flat-leaf parsley

Select the **Sauté** setting on the Instant Pot and heat the oil and garlic for 2 minutes, until the garlic is bubbling but not browned. Add the onion and sauté for 5 minutes more, until the onion begins to soften. Stir in the chicken, broth, and shawarma seasoning, using a spoon to nudge any browned bits from the bottom of the pot and working quickly so not too much liquid evaporates.

Secure the lid and set the Pressure Release to **Sealing**. Press **Cancel** to reset the cooking program, then select the **Pressure Cook** or **Manual** setting and set the cooking time for 15 minutes at high pressure. (The pot will take about 10 minutes to come up to pressure before the cooking program begins.)

To make the vinaigrette: While the chicken is cooking, in a small jar or other small container with a tight-fitting lid, combine the oil, lemon juice, vinegar, water, garlic, salt, and pepper, cap tightly, and shake vigorously. The vinaigrette will not emulsify, so you'll need to shake it again before dressing the salads.

When the cooking program ends, perform a quick release by moving the Pressure Release to **Venting**, or let the pressure release naturally. Open the pot and, using tongs, transfer the chicken to a cutting board.

Press the **Cancel** button to reset the cooking program, then select the **Sauté** setting and cook for about 5 minutes, until the liquid reduces and thickens a bit. While the liquid is reducing, using two forks, shred the chicken into bite-size pieces. When the liquid has thickened, return the chicken to the pot, add the lemon juice, and stir well.

In a large bowl, toss together the romaine and spinach. Shake up the vinaigrette, pour half of it onto the lettuce, and toss until evenly coated. Divide the lettuce evenly among the serving bowls. Top with the tomatoes, cucumbers, bell pepper, a dollop of hummus, a pile of chicken, and a sprinkle of parsley. Drizzle the salads with more vinaigrette, or serve the remaining vinaigrette on the side for diners to add if desired.

Pulled BBQ Chicken and Texas-Style Cabbage Slaw

SERVES 6 **PREP** 5 minutes **COOK** 20 minutes **PR** QPR or NPR

per serving (without cornbread)
320 calories
14 grams fat
18 grams carbohydrates
4 grams fiber
32 grams protein

The Instant Pot makes quick work of cooking chicken thighs—ready in just 10 minutes under pressure. Here, I've tossed them with purchased unsweetened or low-sugar barbecue sauce, which won't send your blood sugar on a roller-coaster ride like other store-bought barbecue sauces. The chicken is served with a fresh and crunchy cabbage slaw tossed with a lime and cumin dressing. Go ahead and have a wedge of cornbread alongside for a balanced meal.

CHICKEN

1 cup water

¼ teaspoon fine sea salt

3 garlic cloves, peeled

2 bay leaves

2 pounds boneless, skinless chicken thighs (see Note)

CABBAGE SLAW

½ head red or green cabbage, thinly sliced

1 red bell pepper, seeded and thinly sliced

2 jalapeño chiles, seeded and cut into narrow strips

2 carrots, julienned

1 large Fuji or Gala apple, julienned

½ cup chopped fresh cilantro

3 tablespoons fresh lime juice

3 tablespoons extra-virgin olive oil

½ teaspoon ground cumin

¼ teaspoon fine sea salt

¾ cup low-sugar or unsweetened barbecue sauce (see Note, page 59)

Cornbread (page 156) for serving

To make the chicken: Combine the water, salt, garlic, bay leaves, and chicken thighs in the Instant Pot, arranging the chicken in a single layer.

Secure the lid and set the Pressure Release to **Sealing**. Select the **Poultry**, **Pressure Cook**, or **Manual** setting and set the cooking time for 10 minutes at high pressure. (The pot will take about 10 minutes to come up to pressure before the cooking program begins.)

To make the slaw: While the chicken is cooking, in a large bowl, combine the cabbage, bell pepper, jalapeños, carrots, apple, cilantro, lime juice, oil, cumin, and salt and toss together until the vegetables and apples are evenly coated.

When the cooking program ends, perform a quick pressure release by moving the Pressure Release to **Venting**, or let the pressure release naturally. Open the pot and, using tongs, transfer the chicken to a cutting board. Using two forks, shred the chicken into bite-size pieces. Wearing heat-resistant mitts, lift out the inner pot and discard the cooking liquid. Return the inner pot to the housing.

Return the chicken to the pot and stir in the barbecue sauce. You can serve it right away or heat it for a minute or two on the **Sauté** setting, then return the pot to its **Keep Warm** setting until ready to serve.

Divide the chicken and slaw evenly among six plates. Serve with wedges of cornbread on the side.

NOTE

If using frozen chicken thighs, increase the cooking time to 15 minutes. Make sure the chicken pieces are individually frozen, rather than a solid block. The recipe also works with chicken breasts, using the same cooking times. If using bone-in chicken, increase the cooking time to 15 minutes for room-temperature chicken or 20 minutes for frozen.

BBQ Turkey Meat Loaf

SERVES 4 **PREP** 5 minutes **COOK** 40 minutes **PR** QPR

Like the BBQ ribs on page 59 and the pulled BBQ chicken on page 69, this recipe calls for a low-sugar or unsweetened barbecue sauce, which means you can enjoy the smoky-sweet flavor of the sauce without worrying about consuming too much sugar. Pair this meat loaf with rice for a comforting meal. I like to round out the dinner plate with bagged frozen mixed vegetables, which are so quick and easy to cook. Microwave the vegetables according to their package directions while the glaze on the meat loaf is broiling.

per serving (meat loaf only)
236 calories
11 grams fat
10 grams carbohydrates
0 gram fiber
25 grams protein

- 1 pound 93 percent lean ground turkey
- ⅓ cup low-sugar or unsweetened barbecue sauce, plus 2 tablespoons (see Note, page 59)
- ⅓ cup gluten-free panko (Japanese bread crumbs)
- 1 large egg
- ½ small yellow onion, finely diced
- 1 garlic clove, minced
- ½ teaspoon fine sea salt
- ½ teaspoon freshly ground black pepper
- Cooked cauliflower "rice" or brown rice for serving

Pour 1 cup water into the Instant Pot. Lightly grease a 7 by 3-inch round cake pan or a 5½ by 3-inch loaf pan with olive oil or coat with nonstick cooking spray.

In a medium bowl, combine the turkey, ⅓ cup barbecue sauce, panko, egg, onion, garlic, salt, and pepper and mix well with your hands until all of the ingredients are evenly distributed. Transfer the mixture to the prepared pan, pressing it into an even layer. Cover the pan tightly with aluminum foil. Place the pan on a long-handled silicone steam rack, then, holding the handles of the steam rack, lower it into the pot. (If you don't have the long-handled rack, use the wire metal steam rack and a homemade sling as described on page 10.)

Secure the lid and set the Pressure Release to **Sealing**. Select the **Pressure Cook** or **Manual** setting and set the cooking time for 25 minutes at high pressure if using a 7-inch round cake pan, or for 35 minutes at high pressure if using a 5½ by 3-inch loaf pan. (The pot will take about 10 minutes to come up to pressure before the cooking program begins.)

Preheat a toaster oven or position an oven rack 4 to 6 inches below the heat source and preheat the broiler.

When the cooking program ends, perform a quick pressure release by moving the Pressure Release to **Venting**. Open the pot and, wearing heat-resistant mitts, grasp the handles of the steam rack and lift it out of the pot. Uncover the pan, taking care not to get burned by the steam or to drip condensation onto the meat loaf. Brush the remaining 2 tablespoons barbecue sauce on top of the meat loaf.

Broil the meat loaf for a few minutes, just until the glaze becomes bubbly and browned. Cut the meat loaf into slices and serve hot, with the cauliflower "rice" alongside.

Unstuffed Peppers with Ground Turkey and Quinoa

SERVES 8 **PREP** 0 minute **COOK** 35 minutes **PR** 15 minutes NPR

per serving

320 calories
14 grams fat
23 grams carbohydrates
3 grams fiber
27 grams protein

The Cajun holy trinity of onions, bell peppers, and celery makes its way into this easy casserole-style dish of high-protein ground turkey and low-carb quinoa, in place of the usual white rice. Much easier to make than stuffed peppers, this one-pot dinner layers everything together in the Instant Pot. The colorful blend is spiced with Cajun seasoning and with a little cayenne for a touch of spicy heat.

---

2 tablespoons extra-virgin olive oil

1 yellow onion, diced

2 celery stalks, diced

2 garlic cloves, chopped

2 pounds 93 percent lean ground turkey

2 teaspoons Cajun seasoning blend (plus 1 teaspoon fine sea salt if using a salt-free blend)

½ teaspoon freshly ground black pepper

¼ teaspoon cayenne pepper

1 cup quinoa, rinsed

1 cup low-sodium chicken broth (see page 148)

One 14½-ounce can fire-roasted diced tomatoes and their liquid

3 red, orange, and/or yellow bell peppers, seeded and cut into 1-inch squares

1 green onion, white and green parts, thinly sliced

1½ tablespoons chopped fresh flat-leaf parsley

Hot sauce (such as Crystal or Frank's RedHot) for serving

Select the **Sauté** setting on the Instant Pot and heat the oil for 2 minutes. Add the onion, celery, and garlic and sauté for about 4 minutes, until the onion begins to soften. Add the turkey, Cajun seasoning, black pepper, and cayenne and sauté, using a wooden spoon or spatula to break up the meat as it cooks, for about 6 minutes, until cooked through and no streaks of pink remain.

Sprinkle the quinoa over the turkey in an even layer. Pour the broth and the diced tomatoes and their liquid over the quinoa, spreading the tomatoes on top. Sprinkle the bell peppers over the top in an even layer.

Secure the lid and set the Pressure Release to **Sealing**. Press the **Cancel** button to reset the cooking program, then select the **Pressure Cook** or **Manual** setting and set the cooking time for 8 minutes at high pressure. (The pot will take about 15 minutes to come up to pressure before the cooking program begins.)

When the cooking program ends, let the pressure release naturally for at least 15 minutes, then move the Pressure Release to **Venting** to release any remaining steam. Open the pot and sprinkle the green onion and parsley over the top in an even layer.

Spoon the unstuffed peppers into bowls, making sure to dig down to the bottom of the pot so each person gets an equal amount of peppers, quinoa, and meat. Serve hot, with hot sauce on the side.

NOTES

For a heartier meal, top each serving with a fried egg or a sprinkle of (dairy or nondairy) cheese.

For a Mexican variation, stir 1 chipotle chile in adobo sauce, minced, into the broth before pouring it into the pot. Substitute 2 teaspoons chili powder and 1 teaspoon salt for the Cajun seasoning and cayenne pepper and use cilantro in place of the parsley. Serve with lime wedges.

Ground Turkey Tetrazzini

SERVES 6 **PREP** 5 minutes **COOK** 20 minutes **PR** 5 minutes NPR **COOL** 2 minutes

There's no need to wait until the day after Thanksgiving to make turkey Tetrazzini from leftover roast turkey. Instead, you can just pick up ground turkey from the store and have it for a weeknight dinner anytime. The mushrooms and turkey are cooked along with whole-wheat pasta, and peas are stirred in at the end to take this classic comfort food into healthier territory. The sauce is lightened up on calories, too, with Laughing Cow or Neufchâtel cheese taking the place of cream cheese.

per serving
321 calories
11 grams fat
35 grams carbohydrates
5 grams fiber
26 grams protein

- 1 tablespoon extra-virgin olive oil
- 2 garlic cloves, minced
- 1 yellow onion, diced
- 8 ounces cremini or button mushrooms, sliced
- ½ teaspoon fine sea salt
- ¼ teaspoon freshly ground black pepper
- 1 pound 93 percent lean ground turkey
- 1 teaspoon poultry seasoning
- 6 ounces whole-grain extra-broad egg-white pasta (such as No Yolks brand) or whole-wheat elbow pasta
- 2 cups low-sodium chicken broth (see page 148)
- 1½ cups frozen green peas, thawed
- 3 cups baby spinach
- Three ¾-ounce wedges Laughing Cow creamy light Swiss cheese, or 2 tablespoons Neufchâtel cheese, at room temperature
- ⅓ cup grated Parmesan cheese
- 1 tablespoon chopped fresh flat-leaf parsley

Select the **Sauté** setting on the Instant Pot and heat the oil and garlic for 2 minutes, until the garlic is bubbling but not browned. Add the onion, mushrooms, salt, and pepper and sauté for about 5 minutes, until the mushrooms have wilted and begun to give up their liquid. Add the turkey and poultry seasoning and sauté, using a wooden spoon or spatula to break up the meat as it cooks, for about 4 minutes more, until cooked through and no streaks of pink remain.

Stir in the pasta. Pour in the broth and use the spoon or spatula to nudge the pasta into the liquid as much as possible. It's fine if some pieces are not completely submerged.

Secure the lid and set the Pressure Release to **Sealing**. Press the **Cancel** button to reset the cooking program, then select the **Pressure Cook** or **Manual** setting and set the cooking time for 5 minutes at high pressure. (The pot will take about 5 minutes to come up to pressure before the cooking program begins.)

When the cooking program ends, let the pressure release naturally for 5 minutes, then move the Pressure Release to **Venting** to release any remaining steam. Open the pot and stir in the peas, spinach, Laughing Cow cheese, and Parmesan. Let stand for 2 minutes, then stir the mixture once more.

Ladle into bowls or onto plates and sprinkle with the parsley. Serve right away.

5

Fish and Seafood

Lemon Pepper Tilapia with Broccoli and Carrots

SERVES 4 **PREP** 0 minute **COOK** 15 minutes **PR** 10 minutes NPR

per serving
243 calories
9 grams fat
15 grams carbohydrates
5 grams fiber
28 grams protein

Tilapia is a mild-flavored crowd-pleaser of a fish and is often the most inexpensive seafood option at the grocery store. Cook it in the Instant Pot with some broccoli and carrots and you've got yourself one of the fastest pressure-cooked dishes around. Serve with Steamed Spaghetti Squash (page 155), brown rice, or whole-grain bread for a balanced meal.

- 1 pound tilapia fillets
- 1 teaspoon lemon pepper seasoning
- ¼ teaspoon fine sea salt
- 2 tablespoons extra-virgin olive oil
- 2 garlic cloves, minced
- 1 small yellow onion, sliced
- ½ cup low-sodium vegetable broth (see page 150)
- 2 tablespoons fresh lemon juice
- 1 pound broccoli crowns, cut into bite-size florets
- 8 ounces carrots, cut into ¼-inch thick rounds

Sprinkle the tilapia fillets all over with the lemon pepper seasoning and salt.

Select the **Sauté** setting on the Instant Pot and heat the oil and garlic for 2 minutes, until the garlic is bubbling but not browned. Add the onion and sauté for about 3 minutes more, until it begins to soften.

Pour in the broth and lemon juice, then use a wooden spoon to nudge any browned bits from the bottom of the pot. Using tongs, add the fish fillets to the pot in a single layer; it's fine if they overlap slightly. Place the broccoli and carrots on top.

Secure the lid and set the Pressure Release to **Sealing**. Press the **Cancel** button to reset the cooking program, then select the **Pressure Cook** or **Manual** setting and set the cooking time for 1 minute at low pressure. (The pot will take about 10 minutes to come up to pressure before the cooking program begins.)

When the cooking program ends, let the pressure release naturally for 10 minutes (don't open the pot before the 10 minutes are up, even if the float valve has gone down), then move the Pressure Release to **Venting** to release any remaining steam. Open the pot. Use a fish spatula to transfer the vegetables and fillets to plates. Serve right away.

Salade Niçoise with Oil-Packed Tuna

SERVES 4 **PREP** 5 minutes **COOK** 20 minutes **PR** QPR

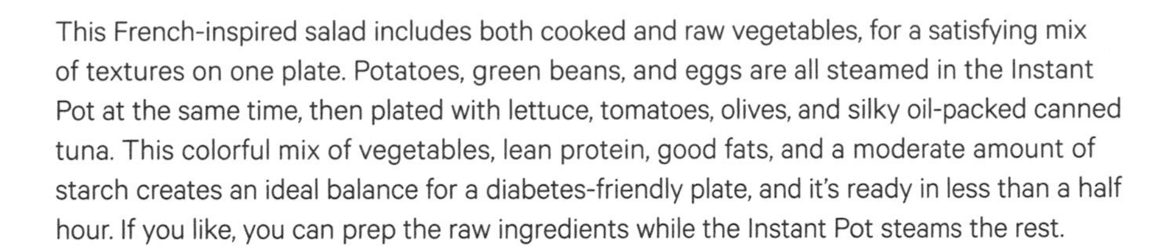

This French-inspired salad includes both cooked and raw vegetables, for a satisfying mix of textures on one plate. Potatoes, green beans, and eggs are all steamed in the Instant Pot at the same time, then plated with lettuce, tomatoes, olives, and silky oil-packed canned tuna. This colorful mix of vegetables, lean protein, good fats, and a moderate amount of starch creates an ideal balance for a diabetes-friendly plate, and it's ready in less than a half hour. If you like, you can prep the raw ingredients while the Instant Pot steams the rest.

per serving

367 calories
23 grams fat
23 grams carbohydrates
4 grams fiber
20 grams protein

8 ounces small red potatoes, quartered

8 ounces green beans, trimmed

4 large eggs

FRENCH VINAIGRETTE

2 tablespoons extra-virgin olive oil

2 tablespoons cold-pressed avocado oil

2 tablespoons white wine vinegar

1 tablespoon water

1 teaspoon Dijon mustard

½ teaspoon dried oregano

¼ teaspoon fine sea salt

1 tablespoon minced shallot

2 hearts romaine lettuce, leaves separated and torn into bite-size pieces

½ cup grape tomatoes, halved

¼ cup pitted Niçoise or Greek olives

One 7-ounce can oil-packed tuna, drained and flaked

Freshly ground black pepper

1 tablespoon chopped fresh flat-leaf parsley

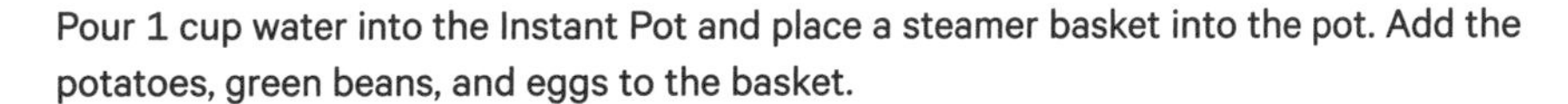

Pour 1 cup water into the Instant Pot and place a steamer basket into the pot. Add the potatoes, green beans, and eggs to the basket.

Secure the lid and set the Pressure Release to **Sealing**. Select the **Steam** setting and set the cooking time for 3 minutes at high pressure. (The pot will take about 15 minutes to come up to pressure before the cooking program begins.)

To make the vinaigrette: While the vegetables and eggs are steaming, in a small jar or other small container with a tight-fitting lid, combine the olive oil, avocado oil, vinegar, water, mustard, oregano, salt, and shallot and shake vigorously to emulsify. Set aside.

Prepare an ice bath.

When the cooking program ends, perform a quick release by moving the Pressure Release to **Venting**. Open the pot and, wearing heat-resistant mitts, lift out the steamer basket. Using tongs, transfer the eggs and green beans to the ice bath, leaving the potatoes in the steamer basket.

While the eggs and green beans are cooling, divide the lettuce, tomatoes, olives, and tuna among four shallow individual bowls. Drain the eggs and green beans. Peel and halve the eggs lengthwise, then arrange them on the salads along with the green beans and potatoes.

Spoon the vinaigrette over the salads and sprinkle with the pepper and parsley. Serve right away.

Shrimp Louie Salad with Thousand Island Dressing

SERVES 4 **PREP** 5 minutes **COOK** 20 minutes **PR** QPR, 5 minutes NPR **COOL** 10 minutes

per serving
407 calories
23 grams fat
14 grams carbohydrates
6 grams fiber
35 grams protein

For celebratory family meals, my parents would often take us to Scoma's Restaurant in San Francisco to enjoy oversize bowls of shrimp Louie salad, piled high with crunchy vegetables and bay shrimp and finished with a creamy dressing. It's a healthful, low-carb meal that still feels luxurious, especially for a summer lunch or dinner. This version includes medium-size shrimp, which cook quickly in the Instant Pot. I always keep a bag of shrimp in the freezer, ready to thaw when the craving for this salad strikes.

2 cups water

1½ teaspoons fine sea salt

1 pound medium shrimp, peeled and deveined

4 large eggs

THOUSAND ISLAND DRESSING

¼ cup no-sugar-added ketchup

¼ cup mayonnaise

1 tablespoon fresh lemon juice

1 teaspoon Worcestershire sauce

⅛ teaspoon cayenne pepper

Freshly ground black pepper

2 green onions, white and green parts, sliced thinly

2 hearts romaine lettuce or 1 head iceberg lettuce, shredded

1 English cucumber, sliced

8 radishes, sliced

1 cup cherry tomatoes, sliced

1 large avocado, pitted, peeled, and sliced

Combine the water and salt in the Instant Pot and stir to dissolve the salt.

Secure the lid and set the Pressure Release to **Sealing**. Select the **Steam** setting and set the cooking time for 0 (zero) minutes at low pressure. (The pot will take about 10 minutes to come up to pressure before the cooking program begins.)

Meanwhile, prepare an ice bath.

When the cooking program ends, perform a quick release by moving the Pressure Release to **Venting**. Open the pot and stir in the shrimp, using a wooden spoon to nudge them all down into the water. Cover the pot and leave the shrimp for 2 minutes on the **Keep Warm** setting. The shrimp will gently poach and cook through. Uncover the pot and, wearing heat-resistant mitts, lift out the inner pot and drain the shrimp in a colander. Transfer them to the ice bath to cool for 5 minutes, then drain them in the colander and set aside in the refrigerator.

Rinse out the inner pot and return it to the housing. Pour in 1 cup water and place the wire metal steam rack into the pot. Place the eggs on top of the steam rack.

Secure the lid and set the Pressure Release to **Sealing**. Press the **Cancel** button to reset the cooking program, then select the **Egg**, **Pressure Cook**, or **Manual** setting and set the cooking time for 5 minutes at high pressure. (The pot will take about 5 minutes to come up to pressure before the cooking program begins.)

While the eggs are cooking, prepare another ice bath.

When the cooking program ends, let the pressure release naturally for 5 minutes, then move the Pressure Release to **Venting** to release any remaining steam. Using tongs, transfer the eggs to the ice bath and let cool for 5 minutes.

To make the dressing: In a small bowl, stir together the ketchup, mayonnaise, lemon juice, Worcestershire sauce, cayenne, ¼ teaspoon black pepper, and green onions.

Arrange the lettuce, cucumber, radishes, tomatoes, and avocado on individual plates or in large, shallow individual bowls. Mound the cooked shrimp in the center of each salad. Peel the eggs, quarter them lengthwise, and place the quarters around the shrimp.

Spoon the dressing over the salads and top with additional black pepper. Serve right away.

Whole-Wheat Pasta Primavera with Shrimp

SERVES 6 **PREP** 0 minute **COOK** 25 minutes **PR** 5 minutes NPR

Pasta is one of the trickier foods to navigate when following a diabetes diet regimen, but it can be done. The best strategy is to bulk up any pasta dish with lots of vegetables and protein, so the noodles themselves aren't the main event on the plate. Here, what would typically be four servings of whole-grain pasta is stretched to six servings when tossed with generous amounts of baby spinach and cherry tomatoes and a pound of shrimp. Go ahead and mix in more steamed vegetables if you like. Broccoli, zucchini, or asparagus would be great here, too.

per serving
301 calories
6 grams fat
35 grams carbohydrates
6 grams fiber
25 grams protein

2 tablespoons extra-virgin olive oil
4 garlic cloves, minced
1 large shallot, thinly sliced
1 pound shrimp, peeled and deveined
2 cups low-sodium chicken broth (see page 148)
8 ounces whole-wheat penne pasta
1½ teaspoons Italian seasoning
One 6-ounce bag baby spinach
1 cup cherry tomatoes, halved
2 tablespoons fresh lemon juice
¼ cup chopped fresh flat-leaf parsley or basil
¼ cup Vegan Parmesan (see page 96) or grated Parmesan cheese
Freshly ground black pepper

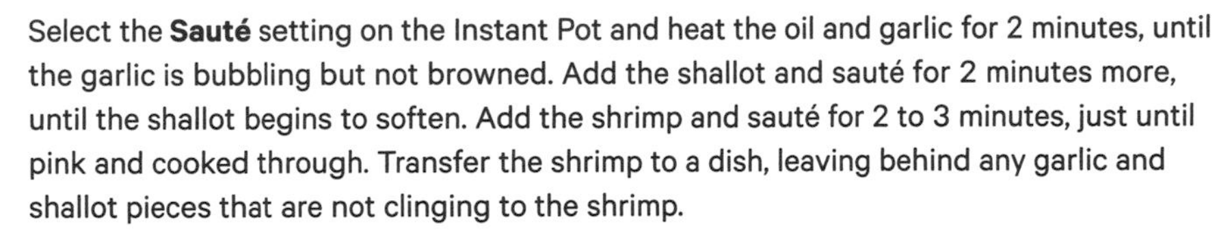

Select the **Sauté** setting on the Instant Pot and heat the oil and garlic for 2 minutes, until the garlic is bubbling but not browned. Add the shallot and sauté for 2 minutes more, until the shallot begins to soften. Add the shrimp and sauté for 2 to 3 minutes, just until pink and cooked through. Transfer the shrimp to a dish, leaving behind any garlic and shallot pieces that are not clinging to the shrimp.

Pour in the broth, then use a wooden spoon to nudge any browned bits from the bottom of the pot. Stir in the pasta and Italian seasoning.

Secure the lid and set the Pressure Release to **Sealing**. Press the **Cancel** button to reset the cooking program, then select the **Pressure Cook** or **Manual** setting and set the cooking time for 5 minutes at high pressure. (The pot will take about 10 minutes to come up to pressure before the cooking program begins.)

While the pasta is cooking, remove the tails from the shrimp, if desired.

When the cooking program ends, let the pressure release naturally for 5 minutes, then move the Pressure Release to **Venting** to release any remaining steam. Open the pot, add the spinach, and stir for about 2 minutes, until wilted. Stir in the shrimp, tomatoes, lemon juice, and parsley.

Spoon the pasta into bowls, sprinkle with the Parmesan and pepper, and serve right away.

NOTE
For a creamy version, stir in two ¾-ounce wedges Laughing Cow creamy light Swiss cheese along with the spinach.

Asian Cod with Brown Rice, Asparagus, and Mushrooms

SERVES 2 **PREP** 5 minutes **COOK** 25 minutes **PR** 5 minutes NPR

per serving

344 calories
11 grams fat
46 grams carbohydrates
7 grams fiber
27 grams protein

Ginger, green onions, and soy sauce flavor both the fish and the brown rice in this Asian-inspired one-pot meal. It's cooked in stackable containers, with the fish and rice in the lower container and the asparagus and mushrooms in the top container. Once you start using this pot-in-pot technique, you'll want to make all kinds of multicourse meals with your Instant Pot.

- ¾ cup Minute brand brown rice
- ½ cup water
- Two 5-ounce skinless cod fillets
- 1 tablespoon soy sauce or tamari
- 1 tablespoon fresh lemon juice
- ½ teaspoon peeled and grated fresh ginger
- 1 tablespoon extra-virgin olive oil or 1 tablespoon unsalted butter, cut into 8 pieces
- 2 green onions, white and green parts, thinly sliced
- 12 ounces asparagus, trimmed
- 4 ounces shiitake mushrooms, stems removed and sliced
- ⅛ teaspoon fine sea salt
- ⅛ teaspoon freshly ground black pepper
- Lemon wedges for serving

Pour 1 cup water into the Instant Pot. Have ready two-tier stackable stainless-steel containers.

In one of the containers, combine the rice and ½ cup water, then gently shake the container to spread the rice into an even layer, making sure all of the grains are submerged. Place the fish fillets on top of the rice. In a small bowl, stir together the soy sauce, lemon juice, and ginger. Pour the soy sauce mixture over the fillets. Drizzle 1 teaspoon olive oil on each fillet (or top with two pieces of the butter), and sprinkle the green onions on and around the fish.

In the second container, arrange the asparagus in the center in as even a layer as possible. Place the mushrooms on either side of the asparagus. Drizzle with the remaining 2 teaspoons olive oil (or put the remaining six pieces butter on top of the asparagus, spacing them evenly). Sprinkle the salt and pepper evenly over the vegetables.

Place the container with the rice and fish on the bottom and the vegetable container on top. Cover the top container with its lid and then latch the containers together. Grasping the handle, lower the containers into the Instant Pot.

Secure the lid and set the Pressure Release to **Sealing**. Select the **Pressure Cook** or **Manual** setting and set the cooking time for 15 minutes at high pressure. (The pot will take about 10 minutes to come up to pressure before the cooking program begins.)

When the cooking program ends, let the pressure release naturally for 5 minutes, then move the Pressure Release to **Venting** to release any remaining steam. Open the pot and, wearing heat-resistant mitts, lift out the stacked containers. Unlatch, unstack, and open the containers, taking care not to get burned by the steam.

Transfer the vegetables, rice, and fish to plates and serve right away, with the lemon wedges on the side.

Mediterranean Salmon with Whole-Wheat Couscous

SERVES 4 **PREP** 5 minutes **COOK** 30 minutes **PR** 5 minutes NPR

Rich in omega-3 fatty acids, salmon is a fantastic choice for a nutritious dinner. I have combined it here with whole-wheat couscous, tomatoes, and zucchini for a Mediterranean-style meal in which everything is cooked together in the Instant Pot. Like Asian Cod with Brown Rice, Asparagus, and Mushrooms (page 82), this calls for two-tier stackable containers, with the vegetables and couscous in one container and the salmon in the other. The gentle heat created with this pot-in-pot method is just what's needed to avoid overcooking delicate fish.

per serving
427 calories
18 grams fat
36 grams carbohydrates
6 grams fiber
28 grams protein

COUSCOUS

1 cup whole-wheat couscous

1 cup water

1 tablespoon extra-virgin olive oil

1 teaspoon dried basil

¼ teaspoon fine sea salt

1 pint cherry or grape tomatoes, halved

8 ounces zucchini, halved lengthwise, then sliced crosswise ¼ inch thick

SALMON

1 pound skinless salmon fillet

2 teaspoons extra-virgin olive oil

1 tablespoon fresh lemon juice

1 garlic clove, minced

¼ teaspoon dried oregano

¼ teaspoon fine sea salt

¼ teaspoon freshly ground black pepper

1 tablespoon capers, drained

Lemon wedges for serving

Pour 1 cup water into the Instant Pot. Have ready two-tier stackable stainless-steel containers.

To make the couscous: In one of the containers, stir together the couscous, water, oil, basil, and salt. Sprinkle the tomatoes and zucchini over the top.

To make the salmon: Place the salmon fillet in the second container. In a small bowl, whisk together the oil, lemon juice, garlic, oregano, salt, pepper, and capers. Spoon the oil mixture over the top of the salmon.

Place the container with the couscous and vegetables on the bottom and the salmon container on top. Cover the top container with its lid and then latch the containers together. Grasping the handle, lower the containers into the Instant Pot.

Secure the lid and set the Pressure Release to **Sealing**. Select the **Pressure Cook** or **Manual** setting and set the cooking time for 20 minutes at high pressure. (The pot will take about 10 minutes to come up to pressure before the cooking program begins.)

When the cooking program ends, let the pressure release naturally for 5 minutes, then move the Pressure Release to **Venting** to release any remaining steam. Open the pot and, wearing heat-resistant mitts, lift out the stacked containers. Unlatch, unstack, and open the containers, taking care not to get burned by the steam.

Using a fork, fluff the couscous and mix in the vegetables. Spoon the couscous onto plates, then use a spatula to cut the salmon into four pieces and place a piece on top of each couscous serving. Serve right away, with lemon wedges on the side.

6

Vegan and Vegetarian Mains

Instant Pot Hoppin' John with Skillet Cauli "Rice"

SERVES 6 **SOAK** 8 hours **PREP** 0 minute **COOK** 30 minutes **PR** 10 minutes NPR

per serving
287 calories
7 grams fat
60 grams carbohydrates
24 grams fiber
23 grams protein

By serving black-eyed peas over cauliflower "rice" instead of white or brown rice, you can significantly lower the carb and calorie count of this classic Southern dish. It's still plenty filling and full of flavor, even with such an improved dietary profile. Black-eyed peas are a nutritional powerhouse, full of magnesium, calcium, and iron along with a good amount of protein and a whole lot of fiber. When flavored with a savory, smoky spice blend and cooked in the Instant Pot, they're just the thing to serve for New Year's Day—or anytime.

HOPPIN' JOHN

- 1 pound dried black-eyed peas (about 2¼ cups)
- 8⅔ cups water
- 1½ teaspoons fine sea salt
- 2 tablespoons extra-virgin olive oil
- 2 garlic cloves, minced
- 8 ounces shiitake mushrooms, stemmed and chopped, or cremini mushrooms, chopped
- 1 small yellow onion, diced
- 1 green bell pepper, seeded and diced
- 2 celery stalks, diced
- 2 jalapeño chiles, seeded and diced
- ½ teaspoon smoked paprika
- ½ teaspoon dried thyme
- ½ teaspoon dried sage
- ¼ teaspoon cayenne pepper
- 2 cups low-sodium vegetable broth (see page 150)

To make the Hoppin' John: In a large bowl, combine the black-eyed peas, 8 cups of the water, and 1 teaspoon of the salt and stir to dissolve the salt. Let soak for at least 8 hours or up to overnight.

Select the **Sauté** setting on the Instant Pot and heat the oil and garlic for 3 minutes, until the garlic is bubbling but not browned. Add the mushrooms and the remaining ½ teaspoon salt and sauté for 5 minutes, until the mushrooms have wilted and begun to give up their liquid. Add the onion, bell pepper, celery, and jalapeños and sauté for 4 minutes, until the onion is softened. Add the paprika, thyme, sage, and cayenne and sauté for 1 minute.

Drain the black-eyed peas and add them to the pot along with the broth and remaining ⅔ cup water. The liquid should just barely cover the beans. (Add an additional splash of water if needed.)

Secure the lid and set the Pressure Release to **Sealing**. Press the **Cancel** button to reset the cooking program, then select the **Bean/Chili**, **Pressure Cook**, or **Manual** setting and set the cooking time for 5 minutes at high pressure. (The pot will take about 10 minutes to come up to pressure before the cooking program begins.)

When the cooking program ends, let the pressure release naturally for 10 minutes, then move the Pressure Release to **Venting** to release any remaining steam.

To make the cauli "rice": While the pressure is releasing, in a large skillet over medium heat, melt the buttery spread. Add the cauliflower and salt and sauté for 3 to 5 minutes, until cooked through and piping hot. (If using frozen riced cauliflower, this may take another 2 minutes or so.)

Spoon the cauli "rice" onto individual plates. Open the pot and spoon the black-eyed peas on top of the cauli "rice". Sprinkle with the green onions and serve right away, with the hot sauce on the side.

CAULI "RICE"

1 tablespoon vegan buttery spread or unsalted butter

1 pound riced cauliflower

½ teaspoon fine sea salt

2 green onions, white and green parts, sliced

Hot sauce (such as Tabasco or Crystal) for serving

Pra Ram Vegetables and Peanut Sauce with Seared Tofu

SERVES 4 **PREP** 5 minutes **COOK** 20 minutes **PR** QPR

per serving
380 calories
22 grams fat
30 grams carbohydrates
10 grams fiber
18 grams protein

Of all the tasks I use my Instant Pot for, the one I come back to most often is steaming vegetables. It's faster than steaming them in a pot on the stove, and it's a more water-efficient method, too, using just 1 cup water. For this recipe, while a nutritious and colorful mix of carrots, zucchini, broccoli, and cabbage steams in the Instant Pot, you'll heat up a skillet to sear tofu slices until crisp and golden. To complete this light, Thai-inspired meal, you'll make a batch of spicy-sweet peanut sauce for spooning over the tofu—a sauce much lower in sugar than its Thai take-out counterpart.

PEANUT SAUCE

2 tablespoons cold-pressed avocado oil

2 garlic cloves, minced

½ cup creamy natural peanut butter

½ cup coconut milk

2 tablespoons brown rice syrup

1 tablespoon plus 1 teaspoon soy sauce, tamari, or coconut aminos

¼ cup water

VEGETABLES

2 carrots, sliced on the diagonal ¼ inch thick

8 ounces zucchini, julienned ¼ inch thick

1 pound broccoli florets

½ small head green cabbage, cut into 1-inch-thick wedges (with core intact so wedges hold together)

To make the peanut sauce: In a small saucepan over medium heat, warm the oil and garlic for about 2 minutes, until the garlic is bubbling but not browned. Add the peanut butter, coconut milk, brown rice syrup, soy sauce, and water; stir to combine; and bring to a simmer (this will take about 3 minutes). As soon as the mixture is fully combined and at a simmer, remove from the heat and keep warm. The peanut sauce will keep in an airtight container in the refrigerator for up to 5 days.

To make the vegetables: Pour 1 cup water into the Instant Pot and place a steamer basket into the pot. In order, layer the carrots, zucchini, broccoli, and cabbage in the steamer basket, finishing with the cabbage.

Secure the lid and set the Pressure Release to **Sealing**. Select the **Steam** setting and set the cooking time for 0 (zero) minutes at low pressure. (The pot will take about 15 minutes to come up to pressure before the cooking program begins.)

To prepare the tofu: While the vegetables are steaming, cut the tofu crosswise into eight ½-inch-thick slices. Cut each of the slices in half crosswise, creating squares. Sandwich the squares between double layers of paper towels or a folded kitchen towel and press firmly to wick away as much moisture as possible. Sprinkle the tofu squares on both sides with the salt and pepper, then sprinkle them on both sides with the cornstarch. Using your fingers, spread the cornstarch on the top and bottom of each square to coat evenly.

In a large nonstick skillet over medium-high heat, warm the oil for about 3 minutes, until shimmering. Add the tofu and sear, turning once, for about 6 minutes per side, until crispy and golden. Divide the tofu evenly among four plates.

CONTINUED ›

Pra Ram Vegetables and Peanut Sauce with Seared Tofu, continued

TOFU

One 14-ounce package extra-firm tofu, drained

¼ teaspoon fine sea salt

¼ teaspoon freshly ground black pepper

1 tablespoon cornstarch

2 tablespoons coconut oil

When the cooking program ends, perform a quick pressure release by moving the Pressure Release to **Venting**. Open the pot and, wearing heat-resistant mitts, grasp the handles of the steamer basket and lift it out of the pot.

Divide the vegetables among the plates, arranging them around the tofu. Spoon the peanut sauce over the tofu and serve.

NOTES

If the peanut sauce is cold, rewarm it in a small saucepan over low heat for a minute or two, adding a tablespoon or two of water if it has become very thick.

For heartier appetites, double the amount of seared tofu.

Palak Tofu

SERVES 4 **PREP** 5 minutes **COOK** 40 minutes **PR** 10 minutes NPR

per serving
345 calories
24 grams fat
18 grams carbohydrates
6 grams fiber
14 grams protein

High-protein, low-fat extra-firm tofu takes the place of *paneer*, a semisoft cheese, in this vegan take on a popular Indian dish. The tofu is cubed and seared in a skillet, then added to a well-seasoned mixture of spinach, tomatoes, and coconut milk that cooks in the Instant Pot. Frozen spinach makes the recipe fast and easy; you can use it straight from the freezer and have a nutritious meal ready in less than an hour that tastes like it simmered much longer on the stove.

- One 14-ounce package extra-firm tofu, drained
- 5 tablespoons cold-pressed avocado oil
- 1 yellow onion, diced
- 1-inch piece fresh ginger, peeled and minced
- 3 garlic cloves, minced
- 1 teaspoon fine sea salt
- ½ teaspoon freshly ground black pepper
- ¼ teaspoon cayenne pepper
- One 16-ounce bag frozen chopped spinach
- ⅓ cup water
- One 14½-ounce can fire-roasted diced tomatoes and their liquid
- ¼ cup coconut milk
- 2 teaspoons garam masala
- Cooked brown rice or cauliflower "rice" or whole-grain flatbread for serving

Cut the tofu crosswise into eight ½-inch-thick slices. Sandwich the slices between double layers of paper towels or a folded kitchen towel and press firmly to wick away as much moisture as possible. Cut the slices into ½-inch cubes.

Select the **Sauté** setting on the Instant Pot and and heat 4 tablespoons of the oil for 2 minutes. Add the onion and sauté for about 10 minutes, until it begins to brown.

While the onion is cooking in the Instant Pot, in a large nonstick skillet over medium-high heat, warm the remaining 1 tablespoon oil. Add the tofu in a single layer and cook without stirring for about 3 minutes, until lightly browned.

Using a spatula, turn the cubes over and cook for about 3 minutes more, until browned on the other side. Remove from the heat and set aside.

Add the ginger and garlic to the onion in the Instant Pot and sauté for about 2 minutes, until the garlic is bubbling but not browned. Add the sautéed tofu, salt, black pepper, and cayenne and stir gently to combine, taking care not to break up the tofu. Add the spinach and stir gently. Pour in the water and then pour the tomatoes and their liquid over the top in an even layer. Do not stir them in.

Secure the lid and set the Pressure Release to **Sealing**. Press the **Cancel** button to reset the cooking program, then select the **Manual** or **Pressure Cook** setting and set the cooking time for 10 minutes at low pressure. (The pot will take about 15 minutes to come up to pressure before the cooking program begins.)

When the cooking program ends, let the pressure release naturally for 10 minutes, then move the Pressure Release to **Venting** to release any remaining steam. Open the pot, add the coconut milk and garam masala, and stir to combine.

Ladle the tofu onto plates or into bowls. Serve piping hot, with the "rice" alongside.

Vegan Dal Makhani

V   

SERVES 6 **SOAK** 12 hours **PREP** 0 minute **COOK** 55 minutes **PR** 30 minutes NPR

per serving
245 calories
7 grams fat
37 grams carbohydrates
10 grams fiber
11 grams protein

Restaurant versions of this northern Indian dish tend to be on the heavy side, with lots of butter and cream. This vegan take is much lighter, and it's partially blended, so you still get a thick, creamy texture. Black-skinned urad dal (aka matpe beans and black gram) are high in protein and fiber, encouraging stable blood-glucose levels. Smaller black beluga lentils and green Puy lentils work great, too. A dollop of coconut yogurt adds just enough richness to each bowl. If you're not in need of a dairy-free recipe, you can substitute unsalted butter for the vegan buttery spread and Greek yogurt (see page 28) for the coconut yogurt.

- 1 cup dried kidney beans
- ⅓ cup urad dal or beluga or Puy lentils
- 4 cups water
- 1 teaspoon fine sea salt
- 1 tablespoon cold-pressed avocado oil
- 1 tablespoon cumin seeds
- 1-inch piece fresh ginger, peeled and minced
- 4 garlic cloves, minced
- 1 large yellow onion, diced
- 2 jalapeño chiles, seeded and diced
- 1 green bell pepper, seeded and diced
- 1 tablespoon garam masala
- 1 teaspoon ground turmeric
- ¼ teaspoon cayenne pepper (optional)
- One 15-ounce can fire-roasted diced tomatoes and liquid
- 2 tablespoons vegan buttery spread
- Cooked cauliflower "rice" for serving
- 2 tablespoons chopped fresh cilantro
- 6 tablespoons plain coconut yogurt

In a medium bowl, combine the kidney beans, urad dal, water, and salt and stir to dissolve the salt. Let soak for 12 hours.

Select the **Sauté** setting on the Instant Pot and heat the oil and cumin seeds for 3 minutes, until the seeds are bubbling, lightly toasted, and aromatic. Add the ginger and garlic and sauté for 1 minute, until bubbling and fragrant. Add the onion, jalapeños, and bell pepper and sauté for 5 minutes, until the onion begins to soften.

Add the garam masala, turmeric, cayenne (if using), and the soaked beans and their liquid and stir to mix. Pour the tomatoes and their liquid on top. Do not stir them in.

Secure the lid and set the Pressure Release to **Sealing**. Press the **Cancel** button to reset the cooking program, then select the **Pressure Cook** or **Manual** setting and set the cooking time for 30 minutes at high pressure. (The pot will take about 15 minutes to come up to pressure before the cooking program begins.)

When the cooking program ends, let the pressure release naturally for 30 minutes, then move the Pressure Release to **Venting** to release any remaining steam. Open the pot and stir to combine, then stir in the buttery spread. If you prefer a smoother texture, ladle 1½ cups of the dal into a blender and blend until smooth, about 30 seconds, then stir the blended mixture into the rest of the dal in the pot.

Spoon the cauliflower "rice" into bowls and ladle the dal on top. Sprinkle with the cilantro, top with a dollop of coconut yogurt, and serve.

No-Bake Spaghetti Squash Casserole

SERVES 6 **PREP** 10 minutes **COOK** 45 minutes **PR** QPR **COOL** 5 minutes

This vegan casserole gets it creamy, cheesy flavor from "Parmesan" made from cashews and "ricotta" made from tofu. They each take just a few minutes to whip up in a food processor while the spaghetti squash steams in the Instant Pot. Low-carb, low-calorie spaghetti squash takes the place of pasta, and the "cheeses" and marinara sauce combine to make a flavor resembling baked ziti, no baking required.

per serving
307 calories
17 grams fat
25 grams carbohydrates
5 grams fiber
16 grams protein

MARINARA

3 tablespoons extra-virgin olive oil

3 garlic cloves, minced

One 28-ounce can whole San Marzano tomatoes and their liquid

2 teaspoons Italian seasoning

1 teaspoon fine sea salt

½ teaspoon red pepper flakes (optional)

VEGAN PARMESAN

½ cup raw whole cashews

2 tablespoons nutritional yeast

½ teaspoon garlic powder

½ teaspoon fine sea salt

To make the marinara: Select the **Sauté** setting on the Instant Pot and heat the oil and garlic for about 2 minutes, until the garlic is bubbling but not browned. Add the tomatoes and their liquid and use a wooden spoon or spatula to crush the tomatoes against the side of the pot. Stir in the Italian seasoning, salt, and pepper flakes (if using) and cook, stirring occasionally, for about 10 minutes, until the sauce has thickened a bit. Press the **Cancel** button to turn off the pot and let the sauce cook from the residual heat for about 5 minutes more, until it is no longer simmering. Wearing heat-resistant mitts, lift the pot out of the housing, pour the sauce into a medium heatproof bowl, and set aside. (You can make the sauce up to 4 days in advance, then let it cool, transfer it to an airtight container, and refrigerate.)

To make the vegan Parmesan: In a food processor, combine the cashews, nutritional yeast, garlic powder, and salt. Using 1-second pulses, pulse about ten times, until the mixture resembles grated Parmesan cheese. Transfer to a small bowl and set aside. Do not wash the food processor bowl and blade.

To make the vegan ricotta: Cut the tofu crosswise into eight ½-inch-thick slices. Sandwich the slices between double layers of paper towels or a folded kitchen towel and press gently to remove excess moisture. Add the tofu to the food processor along with the cashews, nutritional yeast, oil, lemon zest, lemon juice, parsley, Italian seasoning, garlic powder, salt, and pepper. Process for about 1 minute, until the mixture is mostly smooth with flecks of parsley throughout. Set aside.

Return the marinara to the pot. Select the **Sauté** setting and heat the marinara sauce for about 3 minutes, until it starts to simmer. Add the spaghetti squash and vegan ricotta to the pot and stir to combine. Continue to heat, stirring often, for 8 to 10 minutes, until piping hot. Press the **Cancel** button to turn off the pot.

Spoon the spaghetti squash into bowls, top with the vegan Parmesan and parsley, and serve right away.

VEGAN RICOTTA

One 14-ounce package firm tofu, drained

½ cup raw whole cashews, soaked in water to cover for 1 to 2 hours and then drained

3 tablespoons nutritional yeast

2 tablespoons extra-virgin olive oil

1 teaspoon finely grated lemon zest, plus 2 tablespoons fresh lemon juice

½ cup firmly packed fresh flat-leaf parsley leaves

1½ teaspoons Italian seasoning

1 teaspoon garlic powder

1 teaspoon fine sea salt

½ teaspoon freshly ground black pepper

One 3½-pound steamed spaghetti squash (see page 155)

2 tablespoons chopped fresh flat-leaf parsley

Lentil Sloppy Joes

SERVES 6 **PREP** 0 minute **COOK** 40 minutes **PR** 10 minutes NPR

per serving
279 calories
14 grams fat
37 grams carbohydrates
15 grams fiber
13 grams protein

Sloppy Joes get a vegan, lower-carb makeover when they're made with lentils and served open-faced on broiled portobello mushroom "buns." These are definitely a knife-and-fork affair, and they're hearty enough to enjoy on their own as a light lunch or dinner. Add a simple side salad or a wedge of cornbread (see page 156) for a more filling meal. Oh, and the leftovers are great, too: the lentils taste even better the next day, when the flavors have had time to meld and mellow. Make sure to buy vegan Worcestershire sauce. Annie's or Wizard's (by Edward & Sons) are two good choices.

SLOPPY JOES

4 tablespoons extra-virgin olive oil

2 garlic cloves, minced

1 yellow onion, diced

1 red bell pepper, diced

1 carrot, diced

2 celery stalks, diced

1 small Fuji or Gala apple, peeled and grated

1 teaspoon chili powder

½ teaspoon smoked paprika

½ teaspoon fine sea salt

¼ teaspoon freshly ground black pepper

1 tablespoon Worcestershire sauce

1 tablespoon balsamic vinegar

2 cups low-sodium vegetable broth (see page 150)

1⅓ cups green lentils

One 8-ounce can tomato sauce

3 tablespoons tomato paste

To make the Sloppy Joes: Select the **Sauté** setting on the Instant Pot and heat the oil and garlic for 2 minutes, until the garlic is bubbling but not browned. Add the onion, bell pepper, carrot, and celery and sauté for about 5 minutes, until the onion begins to soften. Add the apple, chili powder, paprika, salt, pepper, Worcestershire sauce, vinegar, broth, and lentils and stir well. Pour in the tomato sauce and dollop the tomato paste on top. Do not stir them in.

Secure the lid and set the Pressure Release to **Sealing**. Press the **Cancel** button to reset the cooking program, then select the **Bean/Chili**, **Pressure Cook**, or **Manual** setting and set the cooking time for 25 minutes at high pressure. (The pot will take about 10 minutes to come up to pressure before the cooking program begins.)

To cook the mushrooms: While the Sloppy Joes are cooking, position an oven rack 4 to 6 inches below the heat source and preheat the broiler. Line a sheet pan with aluminum foil.

Brush both sides of each mushroom with the oil, then sprinkle both sides with the salt and pepper. Place the mushrooms, gill-side down, on the prepared pan. Broil for about 7 minutes, until the mushrooms are a bit softened. Turn off the broiler and leave them in the oven to stay warm and continue cooking a bit from the residual heat.

When the cooking program ends, let the pressure release naturally for at least 10 minutes, then move the Pressure Release to **Venting** to release any remaining steam. Open the pot and stir to combine all of the ingredients.

Place the mushrooms, gill-side up, on six plates and ladle the Sloppy Joe mixture over the mushrooms. Top with the onion slices and serve hot.

MUSHROOMS

6 portobello mushrooms, stemmed

2 tablespoons extra-virgin olive oil

½ teaspoon fine sea salt

¼ teaspoon freshly ground black pepper

Thin yellow onion slices for serving

Spinach Salad with Eggs, Tempeh Bacon, and Strawberries

SERVES 4 **PREP** 10 minutes **MARINATE** 2 hours **COOK** 15 minutes **PR** QPR

per serving
435 calories
25 grams fat
25 grams carbohydrates
5 grams fiber
29 grams protein

Even when just one little task is left to the Instant Pot, I find that it simplifies my kitchen routine enormously. Here, eggs are soft boiled in the Instant Pot while you fry marinated tempeh in a skillet. This vegetarian salad is satisfying and high in protein, and the crisped tempeh bacon is a healthier take on the lardons (fatty bacon or salt pork strips) commonly served in this dish.

2 tablespoons soy sauce, tamari, or coconut aminos

1 tablespoon raw apple cider vinegar

1 tablespoon pure maple syrup

½ teaspoon smoked paprika

Freshly ground black pepper

One 8-ounce package tempeh, cut crosswise into ⅛-inch-thick slices

8 large eggs

3 tablespoons extra-virgin olive oil

1 shallot, minced

1 tablespoon red wine vinegar

1 tablespoon balsamic vinegar

1 teaspoon Dijon mustard

¼ teaspoon fine sea salt

One 6-ounce bag baby spinach

2 hearts romaine lettuce, torn into bite-size pieces

12 fresh strawberries, sliced

In a 1-quart ziplock plastic bag, combine the soy sauce, cider vinegar, maple syrup, paprika, and ½ teaspoon pepper and carefully agitate the bag to mix the ingredients to make a marinade. Add the tempeh, seal the bag, and turn the bag back and forth several times to coat the tempeh evenly with the marinade. Marinate in the refrigerator for at least 2 hours or up to 24 hours.

Pour 1 cup water into the Instant Pot and place the wire metal steam rack, an egg rack, or a steamer basket into the pot. Gently place the eggs on top of the rack or in the basket, taking care not to crack them.

Secure the lid and set the Pressure Release to **Sealing**. Select the **Steam** setting and set the cooking time for 3 minutes at high pressure. (The pot will take about 5 minutes to come up to pressure before the cooking program begins.)

While the eggs are cooking, prepare an ice bath.

When the cooking program ends, perform a quick pressure release by moving the Pressure Release to **Venting**. Open the pot and, using tongs, transfer the eggs to the ice bath to cool.

Remove the tempeh from the marinade and blot dry between layers of paper towels. Discard the marinade. In a large nonstick skillet over medium-high heat, warm 1 tablespoon of the oil for 2 minutes. Add the tempeh in a single layer and fry, turning once, for 2 to 3 minutes per side, until well browned. Transfer the tempeh to a plate and set aside.

Wipe out the skillet and set it over medium heat. Add the remaining 2 tablespoons oil and the shallot and sauté for about 2 minutes, until the shallot is golden brown. Turn off the heat and stir in the red wine vinegar, balsamic vinegar, mustard, salt, and ¼ teaspoon pepper to make a vinaigrette.

In a large bowl, combine the spinach and romaine. Pour in the vinaigrette and toss until all of the leaves are lightly coated. Divide the dressed greens evenly among four large serving plates or shallow bowls and arrange the strawberries and fried tempeh on top.

Peel the eggs, cut them in half lengthwise, and place them on top of the salads. Top with a couple grinds of pepper and serve right away.

NOTE

Some varieties of tempeh are higher in carbs than others, and some contain gluten. If you want to go lower carb and/or avoid gluten, choose a tempeh that doesn't contain wheat.

Chile Relleno Casserole with Salsa Salad

SERVES 4 **PREP** 10 minutes **COOK** 55 minutes **PR** 10 minutes NPR

Stirring together all of the components of chiles rellenos to make a casserole is much simpler than making the stuffed, battered, and fried peppers—and it is just as delicious. Because there's no added oil, it is also much better for you. Cut into generously sized wedges and served with a colorful salad, this cheesy, eggy dish makes for a nutritious, high-protein brunch, lunch, or dinner.

per serving

- 361 calories
- 22 grams fat
- 23 grams carbohydrates
- 3 grams fiber
- 21 grams protein

CASSEROLE

½ cup gluten-free flour (such as King Arthur or Cup4Cup brand)

1 teaspoon baking powder

6 large eggs

½ cup nondairy milk or whole milk

Three 4-ounce cans fire-roasted diced green chiles, drained

1 cup nondairy cheese shreds or shredded mozzarella cheese

SALAD

1 head green leaf lettuce, shredded

2 Roma tomatoes, seeded and diced

1 green bell pepper, seeded and diced

½ small yellow onion, diced

1 jalapeño chile, seeded and diced (optional)

2 tablespoons chopped fresh cilantro

4 teaspoons extra-virgin olive oil

4 teaspoons fresh lime juice

⅛ teaspoon fine sea salt

To make the casserole: Pour 1 cup water into the Instant Pot. Butter a 7-cup round heatproof glass dish or coat with nonstick cooking spray and place the dish on a long-handled silicone steam rack. (If you don't have the long-handled rack, use the wire metal steam rack and a homemade sling as described on page 10.)

In a medium bowl, whisk together the flour and baking powder. Add the eggs and milk and whisk until well blended, forming a batter. Stir in the chiles and ¾ cup of the cheese.

Pour the batter into the prepared dish and cover tightly with aluminum foil. Holding the handles of the steam rack, lower the dish into the Instant Pot.

Secure the lid and set the Pressure Release to **Sealing**. Select the **Pressure Cook** or **Manual** setting and set the cooking time for 40 minutes at high pressure. (The pot will take about 10 minutes to come up to pressure before the cooking program begins.)

When the cooking program ends, let the pressure release naturally for at least 10 minutes, then move the Pressure Release to **Venting** to release any remaining steam. Open the pot and, wearing heat-resistant mitts, grasp the handles of the steam rack and lift it out of the pot. Uncover the dish, taking care not to get burned by the steam or to drip condensation onto the casserole. While the casserole is still piping hot, sprinkle the remaining ¼ cup cheese evenly on top. Let the cheese melt for 5 minutes.

To make the salad: While the cheese is melting, in a large bowl, combine the lettuce, tomatoes, bell pepper, onion, jalapeño (if using), cilantro, oil, lime juice, and salt. Toss until evenly combined.

Cut the casserole into wedges. Serve warm, with the salad on the side.

7

Hearty Soups

Manhattan Clam Chowder

SERVES 6 **PREP** 0 minute **COOK** 30 minutes **PR** 10 minutes NPR

Most clam chowder recipes are for the Boston type: cream based and thickened with flour. Manhattan-style chowder is a whole other thing. It's a brightly colored, tomato-based bowl with vegetables, clams, and just enough diced potato to make it satisfying and hearty. Bacon adds a smoky background note that complements the savory, chewy clams.

per serving
191 calories
4 grams fat
24 grams carbohydrates
5 grams fiber
16 grams protein

- 3 slices center-cut bacon, cut into ¼-inch pieces
- 2 garlic cloves, minced
- 1 yellow onion, diced
- 2 carrots, diced
- 1 green bell pepper, seeded and diced
- 2 celery stalks, diced
- 2 teaspoons Old Bay seasoning
- 1 teaspoon dried thyme
- 1 teaspoon freshly ground black pepper
- Two 10-ounce cans baby clams and their liquid
- One 14½-ounce can petite diced tomatoes and their liquid
- 2 cups low-sodium chicken broth (see page 148) or seafood stock
- One 8-ounce bottle clam juice
- 2 bay leaves
- 1 large russet potato, peeled and diced
- 3 tablespoons tomato paste
- ¼ cup chopped fresh flat-leaf parsley

Select the **Sauté** setting on the Instant Pot, add the bacon, and sauté for about 5 minutes, until the bacon has rendered some of its fat and has begun to brown. Add the garlic, onion, carrots, bell pepper, and celery and sauté for about 4 minutes more, until the onion begins to soften. Add the Old Bay, thyme, and black pepper and sauté for 1 minute more. Add the clams and their liquid, tomatoes and their liquid, broth, clam juice, and bay leaves and stir to combine, using a wooden spoon to nudge any browned bits from the bottom of the pot. Add the potato and dollop the tomato paste on top. Do not stir them in.

Secure the lid and set the Pressure Release to **Sealing**. Press the **Cancel** button to reset the cooking program, then select the **Pressure Cook** or **Manual** program and set the cooking time for 5 minutes at low pressure. (The pot will take about 15 minutes to come up to pressure before the cooking program begins.)

When the cooking program ends, let the pressure release naturally for at least 10 minutes, then move the Pressure Release to **Venting** to release any remaining steam. Open the pot and remove and discard the bay leaves. Stir in the parsley.

Ladle the chowder into bowls and serve piping hot.

Cioppino

SERVES 4 **PREP** 0 minute **COOK** 25 minutes **PR** QPR

per serving (cioppino only)
351 calories
10 grams fat
15 grams carbohydrates
4 grams fiber
39 grams protein

This classic San Francisco–style seafood stew is loaded with nutritious vegetables and lean fish, shrimp, and calamari. Purchase bags of frozen seafood blend at the grocery store to keep on hand, and you'll always have the makings for this easy yet fancy-feeling weeknight meal.

3 tablespoons extra-virgin olive oil

1 fennel bulb, quartered lengthwise, cored, and thinly sliced crosswise

2 garlic cloves, chopped

2 shallots, chopped

½ teaspoon fine sea salt

1 teaspoon dried oregano

½ teaspoon red pepper flakes

1 bay leaf

1 cup dry white wine

One 28-ounce can whole San Marzano tomatoes and their liquid

1 pound frozen seafood blend (shrimp, calamari rings, and bay scallops), thawed

1 pound frozen cod fillet pieces, thawed

Chopped fresh flat-leaf parsley or fennel fronds for serving

Gluten-free or whole-grain sourdough bread for serving

Select the **Sauté** setting on the Instant Pot and heat 2 tablespoons of the oil for 2 minutes. Add the fennel, garlic, shallots, and salt and sauté for about 5 minutes, until the fennel begins to soften. Add the oregano, pepper flakes, bay leaf, and wine; bring to a simmer; and cook for 3 minutes. Then stir in the tomatoes and their liquid, breaking them up against the side of the pot a little with a wooden spoon. Bring the mixture to a simmer (this will take about 2 minutes) and stir in the seafood blend and cod.

Secure the lid and set the Pressure Release to **Sealing**. Press the **Cancel** button to reset the cooking program, then select the **Pressure Cook** or **Manual** program and set the cooking time for 0 (zero) minutes at low pressure. (The pot will take about 15 minutes to come up to pressure before the cooking program begins.)

When the cooking program ends, perform a quick pressure release by moving the Pressure Release to **Venting**. Open the pot. Ladle the cioppino into bowls. Drizzle with the remaining 1 tablespoon oil and sprinkle with parsley. Serve piping hot, with the bread alongside.

NOTE

If you do not like the licorice-y taste of fennel (or it is not in season), replace it with 1 yellow onion, quartered and sliced.

Green Chicken Pozole

SERVES 8 **PREP** 5 minutes **COOK** 40 minutes **PR** 15 minutes NPR

per serving
320 calories
14 grams fat
24 grams carbohydrates
8 grams fiber
27 grams protein

The bright, tangy taste of tomatillos distinguishes a green pozole from its tomato-based red counterpart. That translates to a lighter flavor, especially when made with chicken thighs instead of pork shoulder. This fast, weeknight-friendly recipe calls for boneless chicken thighs to speed things up, with no sacrifice in flavor. Topped with crisp cabbage and radishes and a few creamy avocado slices, it becomes a meal in a bowl. Add a crunchy corn tostada alongside if you like.

- 1 large yellow onion, chopped
- 2 garlic cloves, peeled
- 2 jalapeño chiles, seeded
- 2 poblano chiles, seeded
- 1 pound tomatillos, husked, rinsed, and quartered
- 1 cup firmly packed fresh cilantro
- ¼ cup pepitas (pumpkin seeds), toasted
- 2 teaspoons dried oregano
- 2 teaspoons ground coriander
- 1 teaspoon ground cumin
- 1 teaspoon fine sea salt
- 2 cups low-sodium chicken broth (see page 148)
- 2 tablespoons extra-virgin olive oil
- One 25-ounce can hominy, rinsed and drained
- 2 pounds boneless, skinless chicken thighs
- 8 cups shredded green cabbage
- 1 bunch radishes, sliced
- 1 large avocado, pitted, peeled, and sliced
- 2 limes, cut into wedges
- Red pepper flakes

In a blender, combine the onion, garlic, jalapeños, poblanos, tomatillos, cilantro, pepitas, oregano, coriander, cumin, salt, and ½ cup of the broth. Blend for about 30 seconds, until smooth. (Depending on the size of your blender, you may need to do this in two batches.)

Select the **Sauté** setting on the Instant Pot and heat the oil for 2 minutes. Add the tomatillo mixture and cook, stirring often, for about 7 minutes, until it is simmering and has darkened a bit. Stir in the hominy and remaining 1½ cups broth and then add the chicken thighs, submerging them in the liquid.

Secure the lid and set the Pressure Release to **Sealing**. Press the **Cancel** button to reset the cooking program, then select the **Pressure Cook** or **Manual** setting and set the cooking time for 15 minutes at high pressure. (The pot will take about 15 minutes to come up to pressure before the cooking program begins.)

When the cooking program ends, let the pressure release naturally for at least 15 minutes, then move the Pressure Release to **Venting** to release any remaining steam. Open the pot. Using two forks, shred the chicken into bite-size pieces.

Ladle the pozole into bowls and top with the cabbage, radishes, and avocado. Serve hot, with the lime wedges and pepper flakes on the side.

African Peanut Soup with Chicken

SERVES 8 **PREP** 0 minute **COOK** 35 minutes **PR** 15 minutes NPR

Peanuts and chicken are both high in protein, making them ideal candidates for incorporating into a diabetes-friendly soup. This one's spiked with curry powder, coriander, and red pepper flakes for a hit of complex African-inspired spice. The soup is filling enough to be a meal on its own, but I think it's even better ladled over a bed of cauliflower "rice."

per serving

- 355 calories
- 19 grams fat
- 23 grams carbohydrates
- 8 grams fiber
- 29 grams protein

- 1 tablespoon avocado oil
- 1-inch piece ginger, peeled and minced
- 4 garlic cloves, minced
- 1 yellow onion, diced
- 1½ pounds boneless, skinless chicken breasts, cut into bite-size pieces
- 2 teaspoons curry powder
- 1 teaspoon ground coriander
- ½ teaspoon red pepper flakes
- ½ teaspoon fine sea salt
- 3 cups low-sodium chicken broth (see page 148)
- 1 pound carrots, cut into ½-inch pieces
- 12 ounces parsnips, quartered lengthwise, then cut crosswise into ½-inch pieces
- 8 ounces green beans, cut into 1-inch lengths
- One 14½-ounce can fire-roasted diced tomatoes
- 2 tablespoons tomato paste
- ¾ cup creamy natural peanut butter
- 4 cups cooked cauliflower "rice"
- ½ cup chopped roasted peanuts
- ¼ cup chopped fresh cilantro

Select the **Sauté** setting on the Instant Pot and heat the oil, ginger, and garlic for 2 minutes, until the garlic is bubbling but not browned. Add the onion and sauté for 3 minutes, until it begins to soften. Add the chicken and sauté for 3 minutes more, until the chicken is mostly opaque (it's fine if it's not cooked through). Add the curry powder, coriander, pepper flakes, salt, and broth and stir to mix, using a wooden spoon to nudge any browned bits from the bottom of the pot. Stir in the carrots, parsnips, and green beans. Pour in the tomatoes and their liquid and dollop the tomato paste on top. Do not stir them in.

Secure the lid and set the Pressure Release to **Sealing**. Press the **Cancel** button to reset the cooking program, then select the **Pressure Cook** or **Manual** program and set the cooking time for 5 minutes at low pressure. (The pot will take about 20 minutes to come up to pressure before the cooking program begins.)

When the cooking program ends, let the pressure release naturally for at least 15 minutes, then move the Pressure Release to **Venting** to release any remaining steam. Open the pot, add the peanut butter, and stir to combine.

Spoon the cauliflower "rice" into bowls, then ladle the soup on top. Sprinkle with the peanuts and cilantro and serve right away.

NOTE

If you or anyone you're serving is allergic to peanuts, you can still enjoy this soup by substituting almond butter for the peanut butter and chopped roasted almonds for the peanuts.

Chicken Minestrone

SERVES 6 **PREP** 0 minute **COOK** 35 minutes **PR** 20 minutes NPR

per serving
323 calories
8 grams fat
34 grams carbohydrates
9 grams fiber
32 grams protein

Minestrone gets a protein boost from boneless, skinless chicken breasts, making it hearty enough to serve as a main dish. The pot is filled to its maximum capacity line with vegetables, but you'll set the cooking time for only 1 minute, as the soup continues to cook while the pressure is releasing. This is a go-to cold-weather meal for my husband and me. Sometimes I'll add a spoonful of grated Parmesan on top of my bowl, while he likes his dairy-free but with garlic bread on the side.

2 tablespoons extra-virgin olive oil

1 yellow onion, diced

2 carrots, diced

2 celery stalks, diced

½ teaspoon fine sea salt

¼ teaspoon freshly ground black pepper

1½ pounds boneless, skinless chicken breasts, cut into ½-inch pieces

¼ head green cabbage, cored and chopped

2 zucchini, quartered lengthwise, then sliced crosswise ¼ inch thick

8 ounces red potatoes, diced

8 ounces green beans, cut into 1-inch pieces

1½ cups drained cooked cannellini or kidney beans (see page 152), or one 15-ounce can cannellini or kidney beans, rinsed and drained

One 14½-ounce can diced tomatoes and their liquid

4 cups low-sodium chicken broth (see page 148)

1½ teaspoons Italian seasoning

Select the **Sauté** setting on the Instant Pot and heat the oil for 1 minute. Add the onion, carrots, celery, salt, and pepper and sauté for about 5 minutes, until the onion begins to soften. Add the chicken and cook, stirring often, for 3 minutes more, until the chicken is mostly opaque (it's fine if it is not all the way cooked through). Add the cabbage, zucchini, potatoes, green beans, cannellini beans, tomatoes and their liquid, broth, and Italian seasoning and stir well. It's fine if the vegetables and chicken aren't fully submerged, as they will release their own liquid as they cook.

Secure the lid and set the Pressure Release to **Sealing**. Press the **Cancel** button to reset the cooking program, then select the **Pressure Cook** or **Manual** setting and set the cooking time for 1 minute at high pressure. (The pot will take about 25 minutes to come up to pressure before the cooking program begins.)

When the cooking program ends, let the pressure release naturally for at least 20 minutes, then move the Pressure Release to **Venting** to release any remaining steam. Open the pot. Ladle the soup into bowls and serve piping hot.

NOTE

You can also make this recipe with leftover cooked chicken. Cut it into ½-inch pieces and add it with the cabbage and other vegetables.

Beef, Mushroom, and Wild Rice Soup

SERVES 6 **PREP** 0 minute **COOK** 55 minutes **PR** 15 minutes NPR

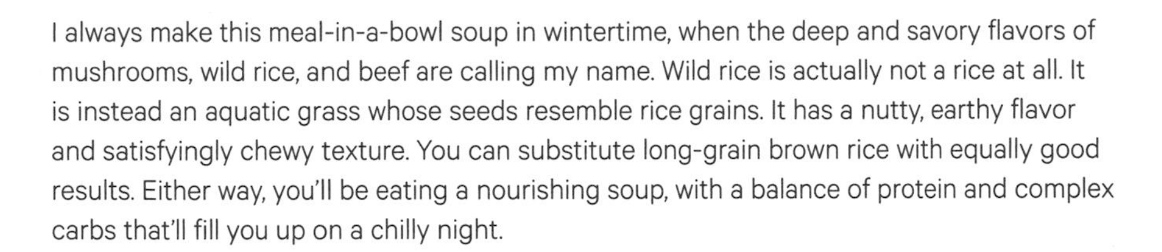
I always make this meal-in-a-bowl soup in wintertime, when the deep and savory flavors of mushrooms, wild rice, and beef are calling my name. Wild rice is actually not a rice at all. It is instead an aquatic grass whose seeds resemble rice grains. It has a nutty, earthy flavor and satisfyingly chewy texture. You can substitute long-grain brown rice with equally good results. Either way, you'll be eating a nourishing soup, with a balance of protein and complex carbs that'll fill you up on a chilly night.

per serving
316 calories
8 grams fat
32 grams carbohydrates
4 grams fiber
29 grams protein

- 2 tablespoons extra-virgin olive oil or unsalted butter
- 2 garlic cloves, minced
- 8 ounces shiitake mushrooms, stems removed and sliced
- 1 teaspoon fine sea salt
- 2 carrots, diced
- 2 celery stalks, diced
- 1 yellow onion, diced
- 1 teaspoon dried thyme
- 1½ pounds beef stew meat, larger pieces halved, or beef chuck, trimmed of fat and cut into ¾-inch pieces
- 4 cups low-sodium roasted beef bone broth (see page 149)
- 1 cup wild rice, rinsed
- 1 tablespoon Worcestershire sauce
- 2 tablespoons tomato paste

Select the **Sauté** setting on the Instant Pot and heat the oil and garlic for about 1 minute, until the garlic is bubbling but not browned. Add the mushrooms and salt and sauté for 5 minutes, until the mushrooms have wilted and given up some of their liquid. Add the carrots, celery, and onion and sauté for 4 minutes, until the onion begins to soften. Add the thyme and beef and sauté for 3 minutes more, until the beef is mostly opaque on the outside. Stir in the broth, rice, Worcestershire sauce, and tomato paste, using a wooden spoon to nudge any browned bits from the bottom of the pot.

Secure the lid and set the Pressure Release to **Sealing**. Press the **Cancel** button to reset the cooking program, then select the **Pressure Cook** or **Manual** setting and set the cooking time for 25 minutes at high pressure. (The pot will take about 15 minutes to come up to pressure before the cooking program begins.)

When the cooking program ends, let the pressure release naturally for at least 15 minutes, then move the Pressure Release to **Venting** to release any remaining steam. Open the pot. Ladle the soup into bowls and serve hot.

NOTE
In this recipe (and in any recipe that includes mushrooms and calls for salt), you can substitute truffle salt for the sea salt to bump up the umami.

Pasta e Fagioli with Ground Beef

SERVES 8 **PREP** 0 minute **COOK** 30 minutes **PR** 10 minutes NPR

While gluten-free pastas can be a little tricky to cook properly in the Instant Pot, I have found that chickpea-based macaroni works well in this hearty Italian soup of ground beef, vegetables, beans, and elbow pasta. Chickpea pasta is higher in protein and lower in carbohydrates than regular wheat pasta, making this soup a lot easier on your blood sugar than traditional versions. Banza is my brand of choice for chickpea pastas and is the easiest one to find in most supermarkets.

per serving
278 calories
9 grams fat
25 grams carbohydrates
6 grams fiber
26 grams protein

- 2 tablespoons extra-virgin olive oil
- 4 garlic cloves, minced
- 1 yellow onion, diced
- 2 large carrots, diced
- 4 celery stalks, diced
- 1½ pounds 95 percent extra-lean ground beef
- 4 cups low-sodium vegetable broth (see page 150)
- 2 teaspoons Italian seasoning
- ½ teaspoon freshly ground black pepper
- 1¼ cups chickpea-based elbow pasta or whole-wheat elbow pasta
- 1½ cups drained cooked kidney beans (see page 152), or one 15-ounce can kidney beans, rinsed and drained
- One 28-ounce can whole San Marzano tomatoes and their liquid
- 2 tablespoons chopped fresh flat-leaf parsley

Select the **Sauté** setting on the Instant Pot and heat the oil and garlic for 2 minutes, until the garlic is bubbling but not browned. Add the onion, carrots, and celery and sauté for 5 minutes, until the onion begins to soften. Add the beef and sauté, using a wooden spoon or spatula to break up the meat as it cooks, for 5 minutes; it's fine if some streaks of pink remain, the beef does not need to be cooked through.

Stir in the broth, Italian seasoning, pepper, and pasta, making sure all of the pasta is submerged in the liquid. Add the beans and stir to mix. Add the tomatoes and their liquid, crushing the tomatoes with your hands as you add them to the pot. Do not stir them in.

Secure the lid and set the Pressure Release to **Sealing**. Press the **Cancel** button to reset the cooking program, then select the **Pressure Cook** or **Manual** setting and set the cooking time for 2 minutes at low pressure. (The pot will take about 15 minutes to come up to pressure before the cooking program begins.)

When the cooking program ends, let the pressure release naturally for 10 minutes, then move the Pressure Release to **Venting** to release any remaining steam. Open the pot and stir the soup to mix all of the ingredients.

Ladle the soup into bowls, sprinkle with the parsley, and serve right away.

Hot and Sour Soup

SERVES 6 **SOAK** 30 minutes **PREP** 0 minute **COOK** 30 minutes **PR** 15 minutes NPR

Here is a comforting first course or snack, especially if you're feeling under the weather. The ginger, white pepper, and chile garlic sauce spice things up, making this my favorite sinus-clearing remedy. With a generous amount of mushrooms and pork loin, the soup is high enough in protein to satisfy and energize.

per serving

231 calories
13 grams fat
14 grams carbohydrates
3 grams fiber
21 grams protein

4 cups boiling water

1 ounce dried shiitake mushrooms

2 tablespoons cold-pressed avocado oil

3 garlic cloves, chopped

4 ounces cremini or button mushrooms, sliced

1 pound boneless pork loin, sirloin, or tip, thinly sliced against the grain into ¼-inch-thick, ½-inch-wide, 2-inch-long strips

1 teaspoon ground ginger

½ teaspoon ground white pepper

2 cups low-sodium chicken broth (see page 148) or vegetable broth (see page 150)

One 8-ounce can sliced bamboo shoots, drained and rinsed

2 tablespoons low-sodium soy sauce

1 tablespoon chile garlic sauce

1 teaspoon toasted sesame oil

2 teaspoons Lakanto Monkfruit Sweetener Classic

2 large eggs

In a large liquid measuring cup or heatproof bowl, pour the boiling water over the shiitake mushrooms. Cover and let soak for 30 minutes. Drain the mushrooms, reserving the soaking liquid. Remove and discard the stems and thinly slice the caps.

Select the **Sauté** setting on the Instant Pot and heat the avocado oil and garlic for 2 minutes, until the garlic is bubbling but not browned. Add the cremini and shiitake mushrooms and sauté for 3 minutes, until the mushrooms are beginning to wilt. Add the pork, ginger, and white pepper and sauté for about 5 minutes, until the pork is opaque and cooked through.

Pour the mushroom soaking liquid into the pot, being careful to leave behind any sediment at the bottom of the measuring cup or bowl. Using a wooden spoon, nudge any browned bits from the bottom of the pot. Stir in the broth, bamboo shoots, soy sauce, chile garlic sauce, sesame oil, and sweetener.

Secure the lid and set the Pressure Release to **Sealing**. Press the **Cancel** button to reset the cooking program, then select the **Pressure Cook** or **Manual** setting and set the cooking time for 5 minutes at high pressure. (The pot will take about 10 minutes to come up to pressure before the cooking program begins.)

While the soup is cooking, in a small bowl, beat the eggs until no streaks of yolk remain.

When the cooking program ends, let the pressure release naturally for at least 15 minutes, then move the Pressure Release to **Venting** to release any remaining steam.

In a small bowl, stir together the vinegar and cornstarch until the cornstarch dissolves. Open the pot and stir the vinegar mixture into the soup. Press the **Cancel** button to reset the cooking program, then select the **Sauté** setting. Bring the soup to a simmer and cook, stirring occasionally, for about 3 minutes, until slightly thickened. While stirring the soup constantly, pour in the beaten eggs in a thin stream. Press the **Cancel** button to turn off the pot and then stir in the green onions and cilantro.

¼ cup rice vinegar

2 tablespoons cornstarch

4 green onions, white and green parts, thinly sliced

¼ cup chopped fresh cilantro

Ladle the soup into bowls and serve hot.

NOTE

If you would like more green, add one 6-ounce bag spinach with the green onions and cilantro and stir just until wilted.

8

Chilis and Stews

Pork Chili Rojo

SERVES 8 **PREP** 5 minutes **COOK** 55 minutes **SOAK** 20 minutes **PR** 20 minutes NPR

Cooking with dried chiles isn't difficult, and the results are rewarding. You simply hydrate the chiles in the Instant Pot and blend them with a yellow onion to form the base of a richly flavored, deep-red sauce. Cubes of pork loin are a leaner choice than pork shoulder, but either will work well here. Serve the chili with a wedge of cornbread (see page 156), a couple warm corn tortillas, or, for a very low-carb option, a scoop of cauliflower "rice."

per serving
242 calories
7 grams fat
10 grams carbohydrates
1 gram fiber
31 grams protein

- 3 cups low-sodium chicken broth (see page 148)
- 2 ounces guajillo chiles, seeded
- 2 ounces pasilla or ancho chiles, seeded
- 1 yellow onion, cut into wedges
- 2½ pounds boneless pork loin roast, trimmed of fat and cut into ½-inch pieces
- 1½ teaspoons fine sea salt
- 1 teaspoon freshly ground black pepper
- 1 tablespoon cold-pressed avocado oil
- 6 garlic cloves, minced
- 2 teaspoons ground cumin
- 2 teaspoons dried oregano
- 1 teaspoon dried sage
- Lime wedges for serving

Add 2 cups of the broth and the guajillo and pasilla chiles to the Instant Pot and cover with the tempered glass lid. Select the **Sauté** setting and set the cooking time for 10 minutes. When the cooking program ends, press the **Cancel** button to turn off the pot, leaving it covered, and let the chiles soak for another 20 minutes.

Using tongs, transfer the chiles to a blender along with the onion. Wearing heat-resistant mitts, lift out the inner pot and pour the broth into the blender. Return the inner pot to the housing. Blend the chile-onion mixture on medium-high speed for about 1 minute, until smooth. Set aside.

Sprinkle the pork all over with the salt and pepper.

Add the oil to the Instant Pot, select the **Sauté** setting, and heat for 2 minutes. Using tongs, add half of the pork in a single layer and sear for about 4 minutes, until lightly browned on one side. Transfer the pork to a plate. Repeat with the remaining pork.

Add the garlic to the empty pot and sauté for 1 minute. Add the remaining 1 cup broth and use a wooden spoon or spatula to nudge any browned bits from the bottom of the pot. Stir in the cumin, oregano, sage, chile-onion mixture, and seared pork and any accumulated juices.

Secure the lid and set the Pressure Release to **Sealing**. Press the **Cancel** button to reset the cooking program, then select the **Meat/Stew** setting and set the cooking time for 20 minutes at high pressure. (The pot will take about 10 minutes to come up to pressure before the cooking program begins.)

When the cooking program ends, let the pressure release naturally for at least 20 minutes, then move the Pressure Release to **Venting** to release any remaining steam.

Ladle the chili into bowls. Serve piping hot, with lime wedges on the side.

Beef and Bean Chili

SERVES 8 **PREP** 0 minute **COOK** 60 minutes **PR** 20 minutes NPR

DF

per serving (without cheese)
340 calories
10.5 grams fat
30 grams carbohydrates
12 grams fiber
33 grams protein

When you choose the ingredients that go into your chili, you can use the leanest ground meat and go heavy on the vegetables to ensure that you end up with a healthful, nutritious meal. Beef and beans are a great combination because you get lots of both protein and filling fiber. Serve the chili on its own or, for a more serious rib-sticking meal, with a slice of cornbread (see page 156).

- 2 tablespoons cold-pressed avocado oil
- 4 garlic cloves, diced
- 1 large red onion, diced
- 2 green bell peppers, seeded and diced
- 2 celery stalks, diced
- 2 teaspoons fine sea salt
- 2 pounds 95 percent lean ground beef
- ¼ cup chili powder
- 2 teaspoons dried oregano
- 2 teaspoons ground cumin
- 2 teaspoons ground coriander
- 1 cup low-sodium roasted beef bone broth (see page 149)
- 1½ cups drained cooked kidney beans (see page 152), or one 15-ounce can kidney beans, rinsed and drained
- 1½ cups drained cooked pinto beans (see page 152), or one 15-ounce can pinto beans, rinsed and drained
- One 28-ounce can whole San Marzano tomatoes and their liquid
- ¼ cup tomato paste

Select the **Sauté** setting on the Instant Pot and heat the oil and garlic for 3 minutes, until the garlic is bubbling but not browned. Add the onion, bell peppers, celery, and salt and sauté for 5 minutes, until the onion begins to soften. Add the beef and sauté, using a wooden spoon or spatula to break up the meat as it cooks, for 6 minutes, until cooked through and no streaks of pink remain. Stir in the chili powder, oregano, cumin, coriander, and broth, using a wooden spoon or spatula to nudge any browned bits from the bottom of the pot.

Pour in all the beans in a layer on top of the beef. Add the tomatoes and their liquid, crushing the tomatoes with your hands as you add them to the pot. Add the tomato paste in a dollop on top. Do not stir in the beans, tomatoes, or tomato paste.

Secure the lid and set the Pressure Release to **Sealing**. Press the **Cancel** button to reset the cooking program, then select the **Pressure Cook** or **Manual** setting and set the cooking time for 15 minutes at high pressure. (The pot will take about 15 minutes to come up to pressure before the cooking program begins.)

When the cooking program ends, let the pressure release naturally for at least 20 minutes, then move the Pressure Release to **Venting** to release any remaining steam. Open the pot and stir the chili to mix all of the ingredients.

Press the **Cancel** button to reset the cooking program, then select the **Sauté** setting and set the cooking time for 10 minutes. Allow the chili to reduce and thicken. Do not stir the chili while it is cooking, as this will cause it to sputter more.

When the cooking program ends, the pot will turn off. Wearing heat-resistant mitts, remove the inner pot from the housing. Wait for about 2 minutes to allow the chili to stop simmering, then give it a final stir.

Ladle the chili into bowls, sprinkle with the cheese (if desired) and green onions, and serve hot.

2 cups nondairy cheese shreds or shredded Cheddar cheese (optional)

4 green onions, white and green parts, thinly sliced

Turkey and Pinto Chili

SERVES 8 **PREP** 0 minute **COOK** 60 minutes **PR** 20 minutes NPR

For a change of pace, try a chili made with ground turkey rather than beef. The spice blend includes coriander and sage, poultry-friendly spices that contribute bright and earthy aromas to balance out the rest of the flavors. While it takes only a little over an hour to make, this chili tastes like it was simmered all day long. I like to use hot chili powder from Penzeys; it delivers just the right amount of heat.

per serving

- 354 calories
- 14 grams fat
- 28 grams carbohydrates
- 9 grams fiber
- 30 grams protein

2 tablespoons cold-pressed avocado oil
4 garlic cloves, diced
1 large yellow onion, diced
4 jalapeño chiles, seeded and diced
2 carrots, diced
4 celery stalks, diced
2 teaspoons fine sea salt
2 pounds 93 percent lean ground turkey
Two 4-ounce cans fire-roasted diced green chiles
4 tablespoons chili powder
2 teaspoons ground cumin
2 teaspoons ground coriander
1 teaspoon dried oregano
1 teaspoon dried sage
1 cup low-sodium chicken broth (see page 148)
3 cups drained cooked pinto beans (see page 152), or two 15-ounce cans pinto beans, drained and rinsed
Two 14½-ounce cans no-salt petite diced tomatoes and their liquid
¼ cup tomato paste

Select the **Sauté** setting on the Instant Pot and heat the oil and garlic for 3 minutes, until the garlic is bubbling but not browned. Add the onion, jalapeños, carrots, celery, and salt and sauté for 5 minutes, until the onion begins to soften. Add the turkey and sauté, using a wooden spoon or spatula to break up the meat as it cooks, for 6 minutes, until cooked through and no streaks of pink remain. Stir in the green chiles, chili powder, cumin, coriander, oregano, sage, and broth, using a wooden spoon or spatula to nudge any browned bits from the bottom of the pot.

Pour in the beans in a layer on top of the turkey. Pour in the tomatoes and their liquid and add the tomato paste in a dollop on top. Do not stir in the beans, tomatoes, or tomato paste.

Secure the lid and set the Pressure Release to **Sealing**. Press the **Cancel** button to reset the cooking program, then select the **Pressure Cook** or **Manual** setting and set the cooking time for 15 minutes at high pressure. (The pot will take about 15 minutes to come up to pressure before the cooking program begins.)

When the cooking program ends, let the pressure release naturally for at least 20 minutes, then move the Pressure Release to **Venting** to release any remaining steam. Open the pot and stir the chili to mix all of the ingredients.

Press the **Cancel** button to reset the cooking program, then select the **Sauté** setting and set the cooking time for 10 minutes. Allow the chili to reduce and thicken. Do not stir the chili while it is cooking, as this will cause it to sputter more.

When the cooking program ends, the pot will turn off. Wearing heat-resistant mitts, remove the inner pot from the housing. Wait for about 2 minutes to allow the chili to stop simmering, then give it a final stir.

Ladle the chili into bowls and serve hot.

White Bean and Chicken Cassoulet

SERVES 6 **PREP** 0 minute **COOK** 30 minutes **PR** 10 minutes NPR

Cassoulet sounds fancy, but it's just a stew of meat and beans. Traditional French cassoulet cooks slowly for hours and hours in a *cassole*, a deep earthenware pot with flared sides, but this Instant Pot version, which combines beans, chicken thighs, chicken sausages, and vegetables, is fast and streamlined enough to serve on a weeknight. Serve the cassoulet on its own or with whole-grain bread alongside.

per serving
296 calories
10 grams fat
20 grams carbohydrates
7 grams fiber
31 grams protein

1 pound boneless, skinless chicken thighs

¼ teaspoon fine sea salt

¼ teaspoon freshly ground black pepper

¼ teaspoon paprika

1 tablespoon extra-virgin olive oil

12 ounces garlic-herb chicken sausages, cut on the diagonal into 1-inch-thick slices

2 carrots, diced

2 celery stalks, diced

1 large yellow onion, diced

1 fennel bulb, cored and diced

4 garlic cloves, chopped

1½ teaspoons dried thyme

2 bay leaves

1 cup low-sodium chicken broth (see page 148)

1½ cups drained cooked great Northern or cannellini beans (see page 152), or one 15-ounce can great Northern or cannellini beans, rinsed and drained

Sprinkle the chicken thighs all over with the salt, pepper, and paprika.

Select the **Sauté** setting on the Instant Pot and heat the oil for 2 minutes. Add the sausages and sear for 4 minutes, stirring once halfway through, until they are a bit browned. Transfer the sausages to a plate.

Add the carrots, celery, onion, fennel, and garlic to the pot and sauté for 5 minutes, until the onion begins to soften. Stir in the thyme, bay leaves, broth, and beans, using a wooden spoon or spatula to nudge any browned bits from the bottom of the pot. Arrange the chicken thighs in a single layer on top of the beans and vegetables. Place the sausages around the chicken thighs.

Secure the lid and set the Pressure Release to **Sealing**. Press the **Cancel** button to reset the cooking program, then select the **Pressure Cook** or **Manual** setting and set the cooking time for 10 minutes at high pressure. (The pot will take about 10 minutes to come up to pressure before the cooking program begins.)

When the cooking program ends, let the pressure release naturally for at least 10 minutes, then move the Pressure Release to **Venting** to release any remaining steam. Open the pot and remove and discard the bay leaves. Stir the cassoulet, breaking up the chicken thighs into large pieces with the spoon or spatula.

Spoon the cassoulet into bowls and serve hot.

Chicken Brunswick Stew

SERVES 6 **PREP** 0 minute **COOK** 30 minutes **PR** 10 minutes NPR

Hearty Brunswick stew is an ideal one-pot dinner for cold nights. It combines chicken, corn, and lima beans in a tomato base, seasoned with a nice dose of hot sauce. My version is fast—you stir in beans and corn straight from the freezer—cooking in just 30 minutes, and the chicken stays in tender, juicy chunks, rather than ending up shredded. The mix of lean chicken and lots of vegetables keeps the dish low in carbs, which means you can pair it with wedges of cornbread, if your carb count allows it.

per serving (stew only)
349 calories
7 grams fat
17.5 grams carbohydrates
7 grams fiber
40 grams protein

- 2 tablespoons extra-virgin olive oil
- 2 garlic cloves, chopped
- 1 large yellow onion, diced
- 2 pounds boneless, skinless chicken (breasts, tenders, or thighs), cut into bite-size pieces
- 1 teaspoon dried thyme
- 1 teaspoon smoked paprika
- 1 teaspoon fine sea salt
- ½ teaspoon freshly ground black pepper
- 1 cup low-sodium chicken broth (see page 148)
- 1 tablespoon hot sauce (such as Tabasco or Crystal)
- 1 tablespoon raw apple cider vinegar
- 1½ cups frozen corn
- 1½ cups frozen baby lima beans
- One 14½-ounce can fire-roasted diced tomatoes and their liquid
- 2 tablespoons tomato paste
- Cornbread (page 156) for serving

Select the **Sauté** setting on the Instant Pot and heat the oil and garlic for 2 minutes, until the garlic is bubbling but not browned. Add the onion and sauté for 3 minutes, until it begins to soften. Add the chicken and sauté for 3 minutes more, until mostly opaque. The chicken does not have to be cooked through. Add the thyme, paprika, salt, and pepper and sauté for 1 minute more.

Stir in the broth, hot sauce, vinegar, corn, and lima beans. Add the diced tomatoes and their liquid in an even layer and dollop the tomato paste on top. Do not stir them in.

Secure the lid and set the Pressure Release to **Sealing.** Press the **Cancel** button to reset the cooking program, then select the **Pressure Cook** or **Manual** setting and set the cooking time for 5 minutes at high pressure. (The pot will take about 15 minutes to come up to pressure before the cooking program begins.)

When the cooking program ends, let the pressure release naturally for at least 10 minutes, then move the Pressure Release to **Venting** to release any remaining steam. Open the pot and stir the stew to mix all of the ingredients.

Ladle the stew into bowls and serve hot, with cornbread alongside.

Alpine Pork and Apple Stew

SERVES 6 **PREP** 0 minute **COOK** 55 minutes **PR** QPR or NPR

This stew is based on dishes from the Alsace region of France, where the stews commonly combine meat and fruit for a sweet-savory main dish. Layers of apple flavor come from apple cider (pick a dry one, as they don't contain as much residual sugar) and from Granny Smith apples, which cook in just a couple of minutes under pressure. Although this dish has a particularly sophisticated taste, it's as easy to make as any everyday stew.

per serving
343 calories
14.5 grams fat
22 grams carbohydrates
5 grams fiber
28 grams protein

- 2 pounds pork stew meat or boneless pork loin roast, cut into 1½-inch pieces
- 1½ teaspoons fine sea salt
- ½ teaspoon freshly ground black pepper
- 2 tablespoons cold-pressed avocado oil
- 1 large yellow onion, chopped
- 3 garlic cloves, minced
- 1 cup dry hard cider or dry white wine
- 1 teaspoon dried thyme
- 1 teaspoon dried sage
- ½ teaspoon dried rosemary
- ¼ teaspoon cayenne pepper
- 1 pound carrots, cut into bite-size pieces
- 2 large Granny Smith or other tart baking apples, each cut into 12 wedges

Sprinkle the pork all over with the salt and black pepper.

Select the **Sauté** setting on the Instant Pot and heat the oil for 3 minutes, until shimmering. Using tongs, add half of the pork in a single layer and sear for about 4 minutes, until lightly browned on one side. Transfer the pork to a plate. Repeat with the remaining pork.

Add the onion and garlic to the pot and sauté for 3 minutes, until the onion begins to soften. Add the cider and use a wooden spoon or spatula to nudge any browned bits from the bottom of the pot. Stir in the thyme, sage, rosemary, and cayenne and then return the pork to the pot.

Press the **Cancel** button to reset the cooking program, then select the **Meat/Stew**, **Pressure Cook**, or **Manual** setting and set the cooking time for 20 minutes at high pressure. (The pot will take about 5 minutes to come up to pressure before the cooking program begins.)

When the cooking program ends, perform a quick pressure release by moving the Pressure Release to **Venting**, or let the pressure release naturally. Open the pot and layer the carrots and apples on top of the pork.

Secure the lid and set the Pressure Release to **Sealing**. Press the **Cancel** button to reset the cooking program, then select the **Pressure Cook** or **Manual** setting and set the cooking time for 2 minutes at low pressure. (The pot will take about 10 minutes to come up to pressure before the cooking program begins.)

When the cooking program ends, perform a quick pressure release by moving the Pressure Release to **Venting**. Open the pot and stir the stew to mix all of the ingredients.

Spoon the stew into bowls and serve hot.

Hearty Hamburger and Lentil Stew

SERVES 8 **PREP** 0 minute **COOK** 55 minutes **PR** 15 minutes NPR

Hearty is the name of the game with this high-protein, high-fiber one-pot meal that marries lentils, vegetables, and lean ground beef. The lentils absorb lots of liquid as they cook under pressure, so you end up with a thick, substantial stew. I like the addition of diced potatoes. You can eat them in moderation on a diabetes-friendly diet when they are combined with fat and protein, and their silky, soft texture really adds to the dish.

per serving
334 calories
8.5 grams fat
30 grams carbohydrates
7.5 grams fiber
34.5 grams protein

2 tablespoons cold-pressed avocado oil

2 garlic cloves, chopped

1 large yellow onion, diced

2 carrots, diced

2 celery stalks, diced

2 pounds 95 percent lean ground beef

½ cup small green lentils

2 cups low-sodium roasted beef bone broth (see page 149) or vegetable broth (see page 150)

1 tablespoon Italian seasoning

1 tablespoon paprika

1½ teaspoons fine sea salt

1 extra-large russet potato, diced

1 cup frozen green peas

1 cup frozen corn

One 14½-ounce can no-salt petite diced tomatoes and their liquid

¼ cup tomato paste

Select the **Sauté** setting on the Instant Pot and heat the oil and garlic for 3 minutes, until the garlic is bubbling but not browned. Add the onion, carrots, and celery and sauté for 5 minutes, until the onion begins to soften. Add the beef and sauté, using a wooden spoon or spatula to break up the meat as it cooks, for 6 minutes, until cooked through and no streaks of pink remain.

Stir in the lentils, broth, Italian seasoning, paprika, and salt. Add the potato, peas, corn, and tomatoes and their liquid in layers on top of the lentils and beef, then add the tomato paste in a dollop on top. Do not stir in the vegetables and tomato paste.

Secure the lid and set the Pressure Release to **Sealing**. Press the **Cancel** button to reset the cooking program, then select the **Pressure Cook** or **Manual** setting and set the cooking time for 20 minutes at high pressure. (The pot will take about 20 minutes to come up to pressure before the cooking program begins.)

When the cooking program ends, let the pressure release naturally for at least 15 minutes, then move the Pressure Release to **Venting** to release any remaining steam. Open the pot and stir the stew to mix all of the ingredients.

Ladle the stew into bowls and serve hot.

Savory Beef Stew with Mushrooms and Turnips

SERVES 6 **PREP** 0 minute **COOK** 55 minutes **PR** QPR

per serving

304 calories
8 grams fat
30 grams carbohydrates
8 grams fiber
29 grams protein

As with my pot roast dinner (see page 54), I like to replace the potatoes in beef stew with other vegetables lower in carbs. Here, a generously portioned mix of mushrooms, carrots, turnips, and parsnips makes for a hearty stew. The rich brown gravy includes a big dollop of tomato paste, which adds body and savory flavor without any added starch. Enjoy the stew on its own, over Steamed Spaghetti Squash (page 155), or following a simple first-course green salad.

1½ pounds beef stew meat

¾ teaspoon fine sea salt

¾ teaspoon freshly ground black pepper

1 tablespoon cold-pressed avocado oil

3 garlic cloves, minced

1 yellow onion, diced

2 celery stalks, diced

8 ounces cremini mushrooms, quartered

1 cup low-sodium roasted beef bone broth (see page 149)

2 tablespoons Worcestershire sauce

1 tablespoon Dijon mustard

1 teaspoon dried rosemary, crumbled

1 bay leaf

3 tablespoons tomato paste

8 ounces carrots, cut into 1-inch-thick rounds

1 pound turnips, cut into 1-inch pieces

1 pound parsnips, halved lengthwise, then cut crosswise into 1-inch pieces

Sprinkle the beef all over with the salt and pepper.

Select the **Sauté** setting on the Instant Pot and heat the oil and garlic for 2 minutes, until the garlic is bubbling but not browned. Add the onion, celery, and mushrooms and sauté for 5 minutes, until the onion begins to soften and the mushrooms are giving up their liquid. Stir in the broth, Worcestershire sauce, mustard, rosemary, and bay leaf. Stir in the beef. Add the tomato paste in a dollop on top. Do not stir it in.

Secure the lid and set the Pressure Release to **Sealing**. Press the **Cancel** button to reset the cooking program, then select the **Meat/Stew**, **Pressure Cook**, or **Manual** setting and set the cooking time for 20 minutes at high pressure. (The pot will take about 10 minutes to come up to pressure before the cooking program begins.)

When the cooking program ends, perform a quick pressure release by moving the Pressure Release to **Venting,** or let the pressure release naturally. Open the pot, remove and discard the bay leaf, and stir in the tomato paste. Place the carrots, turnips, and parsnips on top of the meat.

Secure the lid and set the Pressure Release to **Sealing**. Press the **Cancel** button to reset the cooking program, then select the **Pressure Cook** or **Manual** setting and set the cooking time for 3 minutes at low pressure. (The pot will take about 15 minutes to come up to pressure before the cooking program begins.)

When the cooking program ends, perform a quick pressure release by moving the Pressure Release to **Venting**. Open the pot and stir to combine all of the ingredients.

Ladle the stew into bowls and serve hot.

9

Desserts and Beverages

Chocolate–Chocolate Chip Bundt Cake

SERVES 8 **PREP** 10 minutes **COOK** 50 minutes **PR** 10 minutes NPR **COOL** 1 hour

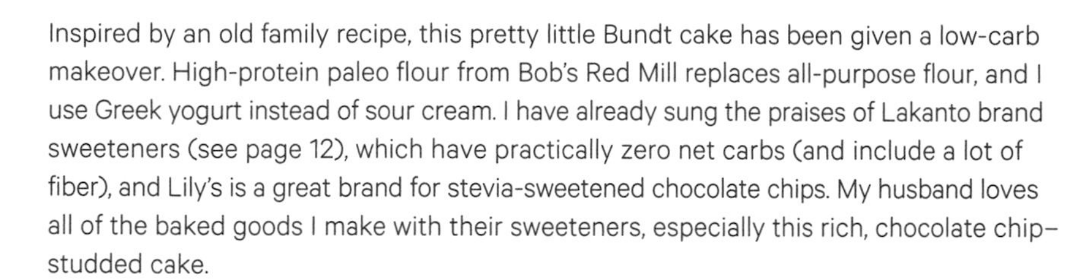
Inspired by an old family recipe, this pretty little Bundt cake has been given a low-carb makeover. High-protein paleo flour from Bob's Red Mill replaces all-purpose flour, and I use Greek yogurt instead of sour cream. I have already sung the praises of Lakanto brand sweeteners (see page 12), which have practically zero net carbs (and include a lot of fiber), and Lily's is a great brand for stevia-sweetened chocolate chips. My husband loves all of the baked goods I make with their sweeteners, especially this rich, chocolate chip–studded cake.

per serving
209 calories
15 grams fat
33 grams carbohydrates
22 grams fiber
7 grams protein

- **1¼ cups Bob's Red Mill paleo flour**
- **⅔ cup Lakanto Monkfruit Sweetener Golden**
- **⅓ cup natural cocoa powder**
- **1½ teaspoons baking powder**
- **½ teaspoon fine sea salt**
- **3 large eggs**
- **½ cup plain 2 percent Greek yogurt (see page 28)**
- **¼ cup vegan shortening or unsalted butter, melted and cooled**
- **1 teaspoon pure vanilla extract**
- **½ cup stevia-sweetened chocolate chips**

Pour 1 cup water into the Instant Pot. Grease a 7-inch Bundt pan with shortening or unsalted butter, then lightly coat the inside of the pan with flour, tapping out any excess.

In a large bowl, whisk together the flour, sweetener, cocoa powder, baking powder, and salt. Add the eggs, Greek yogurt, shortening, and vanilla and whisk just until incorporated. Using a spoon or rubber spatula, fold in the chocolate chips.

Transfer the batter to the prepared pan and, using the spoon or spatula, spread it in an even layer. Cover the pan tightly with aluminum foil. Place the pan on a long-handled silicone steam rack, then, holding the handles of the steam rack, lower it into the Instant Pot. (If you don't have the long-handled rack, use the wire metal steam rack and a homemade sling as described on page 10.)

Secure the lid and set the Pressure Release to **Sealing**. Select the **Cake**, **Pressure Cook**, or **Manual** setting and set the cooking time for 40 minutes at high pressure. (The pot will take about 10 minutes to come up to pressure before the cooking program begins.)

When the cooking program ends, let the pressure release naturally for 10 minutes, then move the Pressure Release to **Venting** to release any remaining steam. Open the pot and, wearing heat-resistant mitts, grasp the handles of the steam rack, lift it out of the pot, and set it on a cooling rack. Uncover the pan, taking care not to get burned by the steam or to drip condensation onto the cake. Let the cake cool for 10 minutes, then invert it onto the cooling rack and lift off the pan. Let cool for about 50 minutes, to room temperature.

Transfer the cake to a serving plate. Cut into eight slices and serve.

NOTE

If you're using another gluten-free flour blend (or all-purpose flour), substitute by weight rather than volume, using 4 ounces flour.

New York Cheesecake

SERVES 8 **PREP** 15 minutes **COOK** 45 minutes **PR** 20 minutes NPR
COOL 2 hours **CHILL** 12 hours

per serving (cheesecake only)

219 calories
17 grams fat
21 grams carbohydrates
13 grams fiber
7 grams protein

This real-deal cheesecake is much lighter on sugar and calories than most versions, so you can enjoy a slice and still feel great afterward. The graham cracker crust is flecked with pecans, and the filling is classic NYC—creamy and tangy sweet—with high-protein additions of Greek yogurt and eggs. In my book, treats should be worth savoring, so rest assured you won't feel like you're missing out on anything with this one. Serve it with fresh berries on the side for a beautiful dessert worthy of company.

CRUST

4 graham cracker sheets (gluten-free, if desired)

¼ cup pecans or pecan pieces

1 tablespoon unsalted butter, melted and cooled

FILLING

One 8-ounce package cream cheese, at room temperature

¾ cup plain 2 percent Greek yogurt (see page 28), at room temperature

½ cup Lakanto Monkfruit Sweetener Golden or Classic

1 teaspoon pure vanilla extract

3 large eggs, at room temperature

1 cup fresh raspberries or sliced fresh strawberries

Line the base of a 7 by 3-inch round removable-bottom cake pan or springform pan with an 8-inch round of parchment paper. If using a springform pan, secure its collar, clamping down the parchment paper and securing the collar onto the base. Lightly butter the sides of the pan or coat with nonstick cooking spray.

To make the crust: In a food processor, process the graham crackers to fine crumbs. Add the pecans and melted butter. Using 1-second pulses, process until the mixture resembles damp sand.

Transfer the crumb mixture to the prepared pan and press it firmly into an even layer onto the bottom and about ½ inch up the sides of the pan. Wipe out the food processor.

To make the filling: In the food processor, combine the cream cheese, yogurt, sweetener, and vanilla. Process using about five 1-second pulses, just until smooth, stopping to scrape down the sides of the bowl as needed. One at a time, add the eggs, processing with two 1-second pulses after each addition. Do not overprocess the filling, or the batter may overflow the pan and/or you will end up with an overly fluffy cheesecake. Using a rubber spatula, gently stir in any large streaks of egg yolk. It's fine if a few small streaks remain.

Pour the filling into the prepared crust. Tap the pan firmly against the countertop a few times to remove any air bubbles in the filling. Cover the pan tightly with aluminum foil. Place the pan on a long-handled silicone steam rack. (If you don't have the long-handled rack, use the wire metal steam rack and a homemade sling as described on page 10.)

Pour 1½ cups water into the Instant Pot. Holding the handles of the steam rack, lower the pan into the pot.

Secure the lid and set the Pressure Release to **Sealing**. Select the **Cake**, **Pressure Cook**, or **Manual** setting and set the cooking time for 32 minutes at high pressure. (The pot will take about 10 minutes to come up to pressure before the cooking program begins.)

When the cooking program ends, let the pressure release naturally for 20 minutes, then move the Pressure Release to **Venting** to release any remaining steam. Open the pot and, wearing heat-resistant mitts, grasp the handles of the steam rack, lift it out of the pot, and set the pan on a cooling rack. Remove the foil, taking care not to get burned by the steam or to drip condensation onto the cheesecake. Use a paper towel to dab up any moisture that may have settled on the surface. The cake will be puffed up and may look a bit uneven when it comes out of the pot, but it will settle and set up as it cools. Let the cheesecake cool on the rack for about 2 hours, then cover and refrigerate for at least 12 hours or up to 24 hours.

Run a butter knife around the edge of the pan to make sure the crust is not sticking to the pan sides. If using a removable-bottom cake pan, set the pan atop a widemouthed jar or can and gently pull downward on the pan ring. If using a springform pan, unclasp the collar and lift if off. Use the parchment border to tug the cheesecake off the pan bottom and onto a serving plate.

Cut the cheesecake into eight slices and serve with the berries on the side.

Fudgy Walnut Brownies

SERVES 12 **PREP** 10 minutes **COOK** 1 hour **PR** 10 minutes NPR **COOL** 2 hours

per serving
199 calories
19 grams fat
26 grams carbohydrates
20 grams fiber
5 grams protein

As their name suggests, these gluten-free, sugar-free brownies are incredibly moist and chocolatey, with an almost melty texture—if you are a chocoholic, you'll love them. Definitely let them cool completely to room temperature to allow them to set up before serving. It is a step that takes some patience, but you will be rewarded with brownies that hold together when sliced.

¾ cup walnut halves and pieces

½ cup unsalted butter, melted and cooled

4 large eggs

1½ teaspoons instant coffee crystals

1½ teaspoons vanilla extract

1 cup Lakanto Monkfruit Sweetener Golden

¼ teaspoon fine sea salt

¾ cup almond flour

¾ cup natural cocoa powder

¾ cup stevia-sweetened chocolate chips

In a dry small skillet over medium heat, toast the walnuts, stirring often, for about 5 minutes, until golden. Transfer the walnuts to a bowl to cool.

Pour 1 cup water into the Instant Pot. Line the base of a 7 by 3-inch round cake pan with a circle of parchment paper. Butter the sides of the pan and the parchment or coat with nonstick cooking spray.

Pour the butter into a medium bowl. One at a time, whisk in the eggs, then whisk in the coffee crystals, vanilla, sweetener, and salt. Finally, whisk in the flour and cocoa powder just until combined. Using a rubber spatula, fold in the chocolate chips and walnuts.

Transfer the batter to the prepared pan and, using the spatula, spread it in an even layer. Cover the pan tightly with aluminum foil. Place the pan on a long-handled silicone steam rack, then, holding the handles of the steam rack, lower it into the Instant Pot.

Secure the lid and set the Pressure Release to **Sealing**. Select the **Cake**, **Pressure Cook**, or **Manual** setting and set the cooking time for 45 minutes at high pressure. (The pot will take about 10 minutes to come up to pressure before the cooking program begins.)

When the cooking program ends, let the pressure release naturally for 10 minutes, then move the Pressure Release to **Venting** to release any remaining steam. Open the pot and, wearing heat-resistant mitts, grasp the handles of the steam rack and lift it out of the pot. Uncover the pan, taking care not to get burned by the steam or to drip condensation onto the brownies. Let the brownies cool in the pan on a cooling rack for about 2 hours, to room temperature.

Run a butter knife around the edge of the pan to make sure the brownies are not sticking to the pan sides. Invert the brownies onto the rack, lift off the pan, and peel off the parchment paper. Invert the brownies onto a serving plate and cut into twelve wedges. The brownies will keep, stored in an airtight container in the refrigerator for up to 5 days, or in the freezer for up to 4 months.

Almond Butter Blondies

SERVES 8 **PREP** 10 minutes **COOK** 50 minutes **PR** 10 minutes NPR **COOL** 20 minutes

Blondies steamed in the Instant Pot turn out moister and denser than the oven-baked variety. They're also foolproof and impossible to burn when cooked this way, which any novice baker can appreciate! Sweetened with a noncaloric sweetener and sugar-free chocolate chips, they contain just 3 net carbs per serving and a good amount of protein from the almond butter and almond flour.

per serving
211 calories
17 grams fat
20 grams carbohydrates
17 grams fiber
8 grams protein

½ cup creamy natural almond butter, at room temperature

4 large eggs

¾ cup Lakanto Monkfruit Sweetener Golden

1 teaspoon pure vanilla extract

½ teaspoon fine sea salt

1¼ cups almond flour

¾ cup stevia-sweetened chocolate chips

Pour 1 cup water into the Instant Pot. Line the base of a 7 by 3-inch round cake pan with a circle of parchment paper. Butter the sides of the pan and the parchment or coat with nonstick cooking spray.

Put the almond butter into a medium bowl. One at a time, whisk the eggs into the almond butter, then whisk in the sweetener, vanilla, and salt. Stir in the flour just until it is fully incorporated, followed by the chocolate chips.

Transfer the batter to the prepared pan and, using a rubber spatula, spread it in an even layer. Cover the pan tightly with aluminum foil. Place the pan on a long-handled silicone steam rack, then, holding the handles of the steam rack, lower it into the Instant Pot.

Secure the lid and set the Pressure Release to **Sealing**. Select the **Cake**, **Pressure Cook**, or **Manual** setting and set the cooking time for 40 minutes at high pressure. (The pot will take about 10 minutes to come up to pressure before the cooking program begins.)

When the cooking program ends, let the pressure release naturally for 10 minutes, then move the Pressure Release to **Venting** to release any remaining steam. Open the pot and, wearing heat-resistant mitts, grasp the handles of the steam rack and lift it out of the pot. Uncover the pan, taking care not to get burned by the steam or to drip condensation onto the blondies. Let the blondies cool in the pan on a cooling rack for about 5 minutes.

Run a butter knife around the edge of pan to make sure the blondies are not sticking to the pan sides. Invert the blondies onto the rack, lift off the pan, and peel off the parchment paper. Let cool for 15 minutes, then invert the blondies onto a serving plate and cut into eight wedges. The blondies will keep, stored in an airtight container in the refrigerator for up to 5 days, or in the freezer for up to 4 months.

Greek Yogurt Strawberry Pops

SERVES 6 **PREP** 5 minutes **FREEZE** 4 hours

Just three ingredients come together in a food processor to create these just-sweet-enough dessert pops. Make sure your bananas are nice and ripe, so they contribute as much sweetness as possible to counterbalance the tangy Greek yogurt. I like to use a food processor for mixing the frozen banana chunks and yogurt because it helps to keep everything very cold and beats a little extra air into the batter. If you prefer to use a blender, use room-temperature bananas (they'll blend much easier) and combine all of the ingredients in one step.

per ice pop
57 calories
1 gram fat
12 grams carbohydrates
2 grams fiber
3 grams protein

2 ripe bananas, peeled, cut into ½-inch pieces, and frozen

½ cup plain 2 percent Greek yogurt (see page 28)

1 cup chopped fresh strawberries

In a food processor, combine the bananas and yogurt and process at high speed for 2 minutes, until mostly smooth (it's okay if a few small chunks remain). Scrape down the sides of the bowl, add the strawberries, and process for 1 minute, until smooth.

Divide the mixture evenly among six ice-pop molds. Tap each mold on a countertop a few times to get rid of any air pockets, then place an ice-pop stick into each mold and transfer the molds to the freezer. Freeze for at least 4 hours, or until frozen solid.

To unmold each ice pop, run it under cold running water for 5 seconds, taking care not to get water inside the mold, then remove the ice pop from the mold. Eat the ice pops right away or store in a ziplock plastic freezer bag in the freezer for up to 2 months.

Blackberry Cobbler

SERVES 6 **PREP** 10 minutes **COOK** 55 minutes **PR** 10 minutes NPR **COOL** 5 minutes

per serving (cobbler only)
256 calories
19 grams fat
28 grams carbohydrates
20 grams fiber
8 grams protein

Thanks to almond flour and noncaloric sweetener, this dessert is much, much lower in carbohydrates than any cobbler you'll ever order in a restaurant. The blackberry filling is lightly sweetened, and a topping of cinnamon "sugar" adds a final dash of spice. Serve it on its own or top it with a scoop of frozen yogurt or nondairy ice cream for an extra-celebratory treat.

BISCUIT DOUGH

- 1 cup almond flour
- 2 tablespoons Lakanto Monkfruit Sweetener Classic
- 1 teaspoon baking powder
- ¼ teaspoon fine sea salt
- 4 tablespoons cold unsalted butter or vegan shortening, cut into ½-inch pieces
- 1 large egg
- ½ cup plain 2 percent Greek yogurt (see page 28)

FILLING

- 3 cups fresh or thawed frozen blackberries
- ¼ cup Lakanto Monkfruit Sweetener Classic
- 2 tablespoons cornstarch or arrowroot

CINNAMON "SUGAR"

- 1 tablespoon Lakanto Monkfruit Sweetener Classic
- ¼ teaspoon ground cinnamon

Vanilla frozen yogurt, nondairy ice cream, or light ice cream for serving (optional)

To make the biscuit dough: In a medium bowl, whisk together the flour, sweetener, baking powder, and salt. Scatter the butter over the top and, using a pastry blender, cut it into the dry ingredients until the mixture resembles coarse sand and the pieces are no larger than peas. If you don't have a pastry blender, use your fingers to rub the butter into the dry ingredients. In a small bowl, whisk together the egg and yogurt, then add to the dry ingredients and stir with a silicone spoon or spatula just until all of the dough is evenly moistened.

To make the filling: In a 7-cup round heatproof glass dish, toss the berries with the sweetener and cornstarch, coating them evenly.

Using two spoons or a 1½-tablespoon spring-loaded cookie scoop, dollop the biscuit dough onto the berries. Cover the dish tightly with aluminum foil.

Pour 1 cup water into the Instant Pot. Place the filled dish on a long-handled silicone steam rack, then, holding the handles of the steam rack, lower it into the Instant Pot. (If you don't have the long-handled rack, use the wire metal steam rack and a homemade sling as described on page 10.)

Secure the lid and set the Pressure Release to **Sealing**. Select the **Pressure Cook** or **Manual** setting and set the cooking time for 45 minutes at high pressure. (The pot will take about 10 minutes to come up to pressure before the cooking program begins.)

When the cooking program ends, let the pressure release naturally for 10 minutes, then move the Pressure Release to **Venting** to release any remaining steam. Open the pot and, wearing heat-resistant mitts, grasp the handles of the steam rack and lift it out of the pot. Uncover the dish, taking care not to get burned by the steam or to drip condensation onto the cobbler. Let the cobbler cool for about 5 minutes.

To make the cinnamon "sugar": In a small bowl, stir together the sweetener and cinnamon.

Spoon the warm cobbler into bowls, sprinkle with the cinnamon "sugar," and top with the frozen yogurt, if desired. Serve right away.

Masala Chai

SERVES 10 **PREP** 0 minute **COOK** 25 minutes **STEEP** 5 minutes **PR** N/A

This comforting brew of tea and spices is inspired by the masala chai made by Rahul Minhas, who operates the Chaiwalla food cart in Wellington, New Zealand. Ginger and black peppercorns contribute zingy spice, while cloves, fennel, and cinnamon add natural sweetness. Once the chai is ready, you can leave it on the Keep Warm setting of the Instant Pot to keep it piping hot for hours. Add a few drops of liquid sweetener to each mug when you're ready to enjoy it.

per serving
12 calories
1 gram fat
0.5 gram carbohydrates
0 gram fiber
0 gram protein

- 6 Darjeeling tea bags
- 2-inch piece fresh ginger, thinly sliced (no need to peel)
- 2 teaspoons green cardamom pods, gently crushed to release the seeds
- 2 teaspoons black peppercorns
- 1 teaspoon whole cloves
- 1 teaspoon fennel seeds
- 1 cinnamon stick, crushed into pieces
- 6 cups water
- 4 cups unsweetened almond milk (plain or vanilla)
- Liquid stevia drops or your favorite sugar-free vanilla syrup (such as Torani or Monin) for serving

Place the tea bags and ginger into a wire-mesh steamer basket. Set aside.

Select the **Sauté** setting on the Instant Pot and mix together the cardamom, peppercorns, cloves, fennel seeds, and cinnamon. Let the spices heat and toast, stirring occasionally, for about 4 minutes, until the pot displays its "Hot" message and the spices are aromatic. Wearing heat-resistant mitts, lift out the inner pot and transfer the spices to the steamer basket, putting them on top of the tea bags and ginger.

Return the inner pot to the housing and place the steamer basket into the pot. Pour the water over the spices and tea and cover with the tempered glass lid. (The pot should still be on the **Sauté** setting.)

When the water begins to simmer, after 8 to 10 minutes, press the **Cancel** button to turn off the pot. Let the tea steep for 5 minutes.

Uncover the pot and, wearing heat-resistant mitts, remove the steamer basket. Pour in the almond milk, select the **Yogurt** setting, and adjust the heat to **More** or **High** (it will display the word "Boil," but it won't come to a rolling boil). After about 10 minutes, the chai will be piping hot and the pot will automatically turn off. (If your Instant Pot doesn't have a **Yogurt** program, select the **Sauté** setting and heat for 9 minutes.) You can serve the chai right away, or keep it warm, covered, on the **Keep Warm** setting for up to 10 hours.

Ladle the chai into cups and serve hot, letting each person sweeten his or her cup to taste with sweetener. I like to use 8 drops liquid stevia or 1 tablespoon sugar-free vanilla syrup. You can also serve the chai chilled, over ice.

Mexican Hot Cocoa

SERVES 4 **PREP** 5 minutes **COOK** 10 minutes **PR** N/A

Enjoy your hot cocoa with a dash of Mexican flair from cinnamon (and a little pinch of cayenne, if you enjoy its spicy heat). Some studies have shown that cinnamon may help lower blood sugar, with Ceylon rather than cassia the more effective of the two main cinnamon types. I like soy milk for this recipe, which is nice and rich, but any nondairy milk will do.

per serving
104 calories
5 grams fat
8 grams carbohydrates
4 grams fiber
10 grams protein

- 4 cups unsweetened soy milk
- ¼ cup natural cocoa powder
- ¼ cup Lakanto Monkfruit Sweetener Golden
- 1 teaspoon ground cinnamon
- Pinch of cayenne pepper (optional)
- ¼ teaspoon fine sea salt

Pour the soy milk into the Instant Pot and cover with the tempered glass lid. Select the **Yogurt** setting and adjust the heat to **More** or **High** (it will display the word "Boil", but it won't come to a rolling boil). If your Instant Pot doesn't have a **Yogurt** program, select the **Sauté** setting and heat for 9 minutes.

In a small bowl, stir together the cocoa powder, sweetener, cinnamon, cayenne (if using), and salt.

When the cooking program ends, uncover the pot and whisk in the cocoa powder mixture until fully dissolved.

Ladle the piping-hot cocoa into mugs and serve right away, or keep it warm, covered, on the **Keep Warm** setting for up to 10 hours. The cocoa will settle to the bottom of the pot after it sits for a few minutes, so give it a stir before serving.

NOTES

My favorite unsweetened soy milk for this recipe is the shelf-stable, organic version from Trader Joe's. Sold in 1-quart aseptic boxes, it is rich, creamy, high in protein, and low in carbs.

For extra-frothy hot cocoa (and to ensure no lumps), use an immersion blender rather than a whisk to incorporate the cocoa mixture.

10

Broths and Pantry Basics

Low-Sodium Chicken Broth

MAKES 8 CUPS **PREP** 5 minutes **COOK** 1 hour 5 minutes **PR** 40 minutes NPR

per 1 cup
35 calories
0 gram fat
0.5 gram carbohydrates
0 gram fiber
8 grams protein

2½ pounds bony chicken parts (such as drumsticks, wings, necks, and backs)

2 celery stalks, cut into 3-inch lengths

2 carrots, halved lengthwise, then cut crosswise into 3-inch lengths

1 yellow onion, cut into wedges

6 flat-leaf parsley sprigs

1¼ teaspoons fine sea salt

½ teaspoon poultry seasoning

2 teaspoons raw apple cider vinegar

8 cups water

Combine the chicken parts, celery, carrots, onion, parsley, salt, and poultry seasoning in the Instant Pot. Add the vinegar and water, pouring slowly to prevent splashing. Make sure the pot is no more than two-thirds full.

Secure the lid and set the Pressure Release to **Sealing**. Select the **Soup/Broth**, **Pressure Cook**, or **Manual** setting and set the cooking time for 40 minutes at high pressure. (The pot will take about 25 minutes to come up to pressure before the cooking program begins.)

When the cooking program ends, let the pressure release naturally for at least 40 minutes, then move the Pressure Release to **Venting** to release any remaining steam.

Place a fine-mesh strainer over a large heatproof bowl or pitcher. For a clearer broth, line the strainer with a double layer of cheesecloth.

Open the pot and, using tongs, remove and discard the chicken pieces. Wearing heat-resistant mitts, lift out the inner pot and pour the broth through the strainer. Discard the contents of the strainer. Pour the broth into a fat separator to remove the fat, then let the broth cool to room temperature. Alternatively, let the broth cool to room temperature, then chill in the refrigerator until the fat solidifies on top and scoop off the fat from the surface with a large spoon. (To speed up the cooling process, prepare an ice bath and set the bowl in the ice bath for about 15 minutes.)

The broth can be used right away, or stored in an airtight container in the refrigerator for up to 5 days or in the freezer for up to 6 months.

Low-Sodium Roasted Beef Bone Broth

MAKES 8 CUPS **PREP** 15 minutes **COOK** 3¼ hours **PR** 45 minutes NPR

per 1 cup

30 calories
0 gram fat
1 gram carbohydrates
0 gram fiber
6 grams protein

- 2 pounds beef soup bones (such as knucklebones, shanks, or oxtails)
- 2 celery stalks, cut into 3-inch lengths
- 1 parsnip or 2 large carrots, halved lengthwise, then cut crosswise into 3-inch lengths
- 1 yellow onion, cut into wedges
- 1 teaspoon fine sea salt
- ½ teaspoon black peppercorns
- 2 bay leaves
- 1 tablespoon tomato paste
- 1 tablespoon raw apple cider vinegar
- 8 cups water

Preheat the oven to 400°F. Line a large sheet pan with aluminum foil.

Arrange the beef bones in a single layer on the prepared pan. Roast for about 45 minutes, until browned.

Using tongs, transfer the roasted bones to the Instant Pot. Add the celery, parsnip, onion, salt, peppercorns, bay leaves, tomato paste, and vinegar. Slowly pour in the water to prevent splashing. Make sure the pot is no more than two-thirds full.

Secure the lid and set the Pressure Release to **Sealing**. Select the **Soup/Broth**, **Pressure Cook**, or **Manual** setting and set the cooking time for 120 minutes at high pressure. (The pot will take about 30 minutes to come up to pressure before the cooking program begins.)

When the cooking program ends, let the pressure release naturally; this will take about 45 minutes.

Place a fine-mesh strainer over a large heatproof bowl or pitcher. For a clearer broth, line the strainer with a double layer of cheesecloth.

Open the pot and, using tongs, remove the bones. Wearing heat-resistant mitts, lift out the inner pot and pour the broth through the strainer. Discard the contents of the strainer. You can pick the meat off the bones if you like, but it will have given up most of its flavor to the broth. Pour the broth into a fat separator to remove the fat, then let the broth cool to room temperature. Alternatively, let the broth cool to room temperature, then chill in the refrigerator until the fat solidifies on top and scoop off the fat from the surface with a large spoon. (To speed up the cooling process, prepare an ice bath and set the bowl in the ice bath for about 15 minutes.)

The broth can be used right away, or stored in an airtight container in the refrigerator for up to 5 days or in the freezer for up to 6 months.

Low-Sodium Vegetable Broth

MAKES 8 CUPS **PREP** 5 minutes **COOK** 40 minutes **PR** 30 minutes NPR

per 1 cup
36 calories
2 grams fat
2 grams carbohydrates
0 gram fiber
2 grams protein

1 tablespoon extra-virgin olive oil

1 large yellow onion, diced

4 garlic cloves, smashed

2 large carrots, diced

4 celery stalks, diced

2 teaspoons fine sea salt

2 teaspoons tomato paste

2 tablespoons nutritional yeast

8 cups water

1 teaspoon black peppercorns

2 bay leaves

3 ounces flat-leaf parsley sprigs

Select the **Sauté** setting on the Instant Pot and heat the oil for 1 minute. Add the onion, garlic, carrots, celery, and salt and sauté for about 10 minutes, until the vegetables give up some of their liquid and begin to brown. Stir in the tomato paste and nutritional yeast, add 1 cup of the water, and use a wooden spoon or spatula to nudge any browned bits from the bottom of the pot. Add the peppercorns, bay leaves, and parsley and slowly pour in the remaining 7 cups water, making sure the pot is no more than two-thirds full.

Secure the lid and set the Pressure Release to **Sealing**. Press the **Cancel** button to reset the cooking program, then select the **Soup/Broth**, **Pressure Cook**, or **Manual** setting and set the cooking time for 10 minutes at high pressure. (The pot will take about 20 minutes to come up to pressure before the cooking program begins.)

When the cooking program ends, let the pressure release naturally for 30 minutes, then move the Pressure Release to **Venting** to release any remaining steam.

Place a fine-mesh strainer over a large heatproof bowl or pitcher. For a clearer broth, line the strainer with a double layer of cheesecloth.

Open the pot and, wearing heat-resistant mitts, lift out the inner pot and pour the broth through the strainer. Discard the contents of the strainer. Let the broth cool to room temperature. (To speed up the cooling process, prepare an ice bath and set the bowl in the ice bath for about 15 minutes.)

The broth can be used right away, or stored in an airtight container in the refrigerator for up to 5 days or in the freezer for up to 6 months.

Cashew Ranch Dip

MAKES 2 CUPS **BLEND** 1 minute **COOL** 1 hour

per 2 tablespoons
44 calories
3 grams fat
3 grams carbohydrates
0 gram fiber
1 gram protein

1 cup raw whole cashews, soaked in water to cover for 1 to 2 hours and then drained

½ cup water

2 tablespoons fresh lemon juice

1 teaspoon nutritional yeast

1 teaspoon garlic powder

½ teaspoon fine sea salt

½ teaspoon freshly ground black pepper

1 tablespoon chopped fresh chives

1 tablespoon chopped fresh dill

1 tablespoon chopped fresh flat-leaf parsley

In a blender, combine the cashews, water, lemon juice, nutritional yeast, garlic powder, salt, and pepper. Blend on high speed for about 1 minute, until very smooth, stopping to scrape down the sides if needed.

Transfer the dip to a bowl and stir in the chives, dill, and parsley. Cover and refrigerate for at least 1 hour before serving. The dip will keep in the refrigerator for up to 5 days. If it becomes too thick, stir in a splash of water.

Basic Beans

MAKES ABOUT 6 CUPS **SOAK** 10 hours **COOK** varies **PR** 30 minutes NPR

1 pound dried beans, any variety (about 2¼ cups)

8 cups water

2 teaspoons fine sea salt

Combine the beans, water, and salt in the Instant Pot and stir to dissolve the salt. Secure the lid and set the Pressure Release to **Sealing**.

If soaking the beans, select the **Bean/Chili**, **Pressure Cook**, or **Manual** setting, then refer to the Soaked, Cooking Time column in the Beans table on page 158 for setting the cooking time; use high pressure. Next, select the **Timer** or **Delay** function and set the time delay for 10 to 12 hours. (When the soaking time is complete, the pot will take about 20 minutes to come up to pressure before the cooking program begins.)

If not soaking the beans, refer to the Unsoaked, Cooking Time column in the Beans table on page 158 for setting the cooking time; use high pressure.

When the cooking program ends, let the pressure release naturally (this will take about 30 minutes). Open the pot and, wearing heat-resistant mitts, lift out the inner pot. If using the beans immediately, drain them in a colander. If refrigerating the beans, ladle the beans and their cooking liquid into airtight containers, let cool for about 1 hour, then cover and refrigerate for up to 5 days. If freezing the beans, drain them in a colander, let cool to room temperature, spoon 1½ cup portions into 1-quart ziplock plastic freezer bags, seal well, and freeze for up to 6 months.

Tips for Cooking Beans

Cooking 1 pound dried beans will yield roughly the same amount of cooked beans as four 15-ounce cans beans, and you can flavor and season them however you like.

In an ideal world, I'd always remember to soak my beans in salted water for 10 to 12 hours before cooking, as soaked beans typically hold their shape better during cooking. In contrast, unsoaked beans tend to split their skins and sometimes break apart, depending on the variety. Chickpeas are especially forgiving whether soaked or unsoaked, so they're a nice starter legume for anyone new to cooking beans. Refried beans are another easy choice, since mashing them up after cooking disguises any imperfections.

If you prefer to change out the soaking water for fresh water before cooking the beans, feel free to do so. In this case, you'll want to leave the pot turned off up until you drain the soaked beans and return them to the pot. Add fresh water and start the cooking program, skipping the **Timer** or **Delay** function.

Add aromatic ingredients to your pot of beans to take it beyond the basic. Options include a few peeled garlic cloves; a yellow onion, cut into wedges; a bay leaf or two; or a piece of *kombu* (dried kelp). Some sources say kombu, a traditional addition to Japanese dashi, may also help to improve the digestibility of beans.

Steamed Spaghetti Squash

MAKES 6 CUPS **PREP** 5 minutes **COOK** 20 minutes **PR** QPR **COOL** 5 minutes

per 1 cup
42 calories
0.5 gram fat
10 grams carbohydrates
2 grams fiber
1 gram protein

One 3½-pound spaghetti squash

Pour 1 cup water into the Instant Pot and place the wire metal steam rack into the pot.

Trim off the stem end of the squash, cut the squash into quarters, and scoop out and discard the seeds. Place the squash quarters on the steam rack, arranging the pieces in a single layer, if possible, or nesting them inside one another if needed to fit.

Secure the lid and set the Pressure Release to **Sealing**. Select the **Steam** setting and set the cooking time for 7 minutes at high pressure. (The pot will take about 10 minutes to come up to pressure before the cooking program begins.)

When the cooking program ends, perform a quick pressure release by moving the Pressure Release to **Venting**. Open the pot and, using tongs, transfer the squash to a plate or cutting board. Let stand for about 5 minutes, until cool enough to handle. Using a fork, separate the strands of the spaghetti squash. Discard the skin.

Use right away, or let cool to room temperature, transfer to an airtight container, and refrigerate for up to 3 days.

Cornbread

SERVES 8 **PREP** 10 minutes **COOK** 45 minutes **PR** 10 minutes NPR **COOL** 5 minutes

per serving
230 calories
17 grams fat
14 grams carbohydrates
3 grams fiber
6 grams protein

- 1 cup almond flour
- ½ cup cornmeal
- ¼ cup coconut flour
- 2 teaspoons baking powder
- 1 teaspoon fine sea salt
- 2 large eggs
- 1 cup unsweetened almond milk
- 4 tablespoons vegan shortening or unsalted butter, melted and cooled

Pour 1 cup water into the Instant Pot. Grease the bottom and sides of a 7-inch round cake pan with shortening or butter.

In a medium bowl, whisk together the almond flour, cornmeal, coconut flour, baking powder, and salt. In another medium bowl, whisk together the eggs and almond milk until no streaks of yolk remain.

Add the egg mixture and shortening to the almond flour mixture and whisk just until the dry ingredients are evenly and fully moistened. The coconut flour absorbs moisture quickly, so the batter will thicken as it sits.

Transfer the batter to the prepared pan and, using a rubber spatula, spread it in an even layer. Cover the pan tightly with aluminum foil. Place the pan on a long-handled silicone steam rack, then, holding the handles of the steam rack, lower it into the Instant Pot. (If you don't have the long-handled rack, use the wire metal steam rack and a homemade sling as described on page 10.)

Secure the lid and set the Pressure Release to **Sealing**. Select the **Cake**, **Pressure Cook**, or **Manual** setting and set the cooking time for 35 minutes at high pressure. (The pot will take about 10 minutes to come up to pressure before the cooking program begins.)

When the cooking program ends, let the pressure release naturally for 10 minutes, then move the Pressure Release to **Venting** to release any remaining steam. Open the pot and, wearing heat-resistant mitts, grasp the handles of the steam rack, lift it out of the pot, and set it on a cooling rack. Uncover the pan, taking care not to get burned by the steam or to drip condensation onto the bread. Let the bread cool for 5 minutes, then run a butter knife around the edge of the pan to loosen the bread from the pan sides. Invert the bread onto the cooling rack, lift off the pan, and invert the bread onto a serving plate.

Cut the bread into eight wedges and serve warm.

NOTE

If you're craving a sweet topping for your cornbread, ChocZero's maple-flavored, sugar-free syrup mixed with equal parts softened butter makes a great sugar-free spread.

Cooking Charts

Refer to these charts* to determine the cooking times for many different foods. When converting recipes for the Instant Pot, use the longest-cooking ingredient to determine the cooking time.

Meat and Poultry	Cooking Time (in minutes)	Pressure Release
Beef, stew meat	25 to 30	natural
Beef, pot roast, steak, rump, round, chuck, blade, or brisket, large chunks	35 to 40	natural
Beef, pot roast, rump, round, chuck, or brisket, small chunks	25 to 30	natural
Beef, pot roast, rump, round, chuck, or brisket, whole, up to 4 pounds	20 to 25/ pound	natural
Beef, short ribs	30 to 35	natural
Beef, shanks (crosscut)	30 to 35	natural
Beef, oxtail	50 to 55	natural
Chicken, breasts, with bones	10 to 15	quick
Chicken, breasts, boneless, skinless	8	quick
Chicken, drumsticks, legs, or thighs, with bones	15	quick
Chicken, thighs, boneless	10	quick
Chicken, whole	20 to 25	quick
Chicken, whole, cut up with bones	10 to 15	quick
Ham slice	9 to 12	quick
Lamb, stew meat	20 to 25	natural
Pork, loin roast	20/pound	natural
Pork, butt roast	15/pound	natural
Pork, ribs	20 to 25	natural
Turkey, breast, boneless	15 to 20	quick
Turkey, breast, whole, with bones	25 to 30	quick
Turkey, drumsticks (leg)	15 to 20	quick

*Charts adapted from information provided by Instant Pot.

Rice and Other Grains	Water Quantity (Rice/Grain: Water Ratio)**	Cooking Time (in minutes)
Barley, pearl	1:1½ to 2	25 to 30
Barley, pot	1:3 to 4	25 to 30
Congee, thick	1:4 to 5	15 to 20
Congee, thin	1:6 to 7	15 to 20
Couscous (not quick-cooking)	1:2	5 to 8
Millet	1:1⅔	10 to 12
Oats, old-fashioned (rolled)	1:1⅔	6
Oats, steel-cut	1:3	10 to 12
Polenta, coarse	1:4	10 to 15
Quinoa	1:1 to 1¼	8
Rice, basmati	1:1 to 1¼	4 to 8
Rice, brown	1:1 to 1¼	20 to 25
Rice, jasmine	1:1 to 1¼	4 to 10
Rice, white	1:1 to 1¼	8
Rice, wild	1:1⅓ to 1½	25 to 30
Whole-grain wheat berries, spelt, farro, or kamut	1:1½ to 2	25 to 30

**Less water will yield a firmer, more separate grain, while more water will yield a softer grain.

Beans	Soaked, Cooking Time (in minutes)	Unsoaked, Cooking Time (in minutes)
Black	6 to 8	20 to 25
Black-eyed pea	4 to 5	20 to 25
Cannellini	6 to 9	30 to 35
Chickpea (garbanzo)	10 to 15	35 to 40
Corona, gigante	10 to 15	25 to 30
Flageolet	6 to 9	20 to 25
Great Northern	12 to 14	25 to 30
Kidney	7 to 8	15 to 20
Lima	6 to 10	12 to 14
Navy	7 to 8	20 to 25
Pinquito	5 to 7	20 to 25
Pinto	6 to 9	25 to 30
Red	6 to 8	20 to 25

Lentils	Soaked, Cooking Time (in minutes)	Unsoaked, Cooking Time (in minutes)
Beluga (black)	n/a	15 to 20
Green	n/a	15 to 20
Puy (French)	n/a	15 to 20
Red (split)	n/a	15 to 18
Small brown (Spanish)	n/a	15 to 20
Yellow (split)	n/a	15 to 18

Vegetables	Fresh, Cooking Time (in minutes)	Frozen, Cooking Time (in minutes)
Artichokes, whole, trimmed without leaves removed	9 to 11	11 to 13
Artichokes, hearts	4 to 5	5 to 6
Asparagus, whole or cut	0 to 2	2 to 3
Beets, small, whole	11 to 13	13 to 15
Beets, large, whole	20 to 25	25 to 30
Broccoli, florets	0 to 2	2 to 3
Broccoli, stalks	1 to 3	3 to 4
Brussels sprouts, whole	2 to 4	4 to 5
Cabbage, red, purple or green, shredded	1 to 2	2 to 3
Cabbage, red, purple or green, wedges	2 to 3	3 to 4
Carrots, sliced or shredded	1 to 2	2 to 3
Carrots, whole or chunks	2 to 3	3 to 4
Cauliflower, florets	1 to 2	3 to 4
Celery, chunks	2 to 3	3 to 4
Corn, kernels	1 to 2	2 to 3
Corn, on the cob	3 to 4	4 to 5
Eggplant, slices or chunks	2 to 3	3 to 4
Endives, whole	1 to 2	2 to 3
Escarole, chopped	1 to 2	2 to 3
Green beans, whole	3 to 5	4 to 7
Greens (beet greens, collards, kale, spinach, Swiss chard, turnip greens), chopped	3 to 6	4 to 7

Vegetables	Fresh, Cooking Time (in minutes)	Frozen, Cooking Time (in minutes)
Leeks, chopped	2 to 4	3 to 5
Mixed vegetables, chopped (frozen blend)	2 to 3	3 to 4
Okra, sliced	2 to 3	3 to 4
Onions, sliced	2 to 3	3 to 4
Parsnips, sliced	1 to 2	2 to 3
Parsnips, chunks	2 to 4	4 to 6
Peas, sugar snap or snow, whole	0 to 1	2 to 3
Peas, green (English), shelled	0 to 1	2 to 3
Potatoes, in cubes	3 to 5	7 to 9
Potatoes, whole, baby	10 to 12	12 to 14
Potatoes, whole, large	12 to 15	15 to 19
Pumpkin, small slices or chunks	4 to 5	6 to 7
Rutabagas, slices	3 to 5	4 to 6
Rutabagas, chunks	4 to 6	6 to 8
Spinach	0 to 1	2 to 3
Squash, acorn, slices or chunks	6 to 7	8 to 9
Squash, butternut, slices or chunks	6 to 7	8 to 9
Sweet peppers, slices or chunks	0 to 2	3 to 4
Sweet potatoes, cubed	3 to 5	5 to 7
Sweet potatoes, whole, small	10 to 12	12 to 14
Sweet potatoes, whole, large	12 to 15	15 to 19
Tomatoes, quartered	2 to 3	4 to 5
Tomatoes, whole	3 to 5	5 to 7
Turnips, chunks	2 to 4	4 to 6
Yams, cubed	3 to 5	5 to 7
Yams, whole, small	12 to 15	15 to 19
Zucchini, slices or chunks	2 to 3	3 to 4

Acknowledgments

To my husband, Brendan, being diagnosed with type 1 diabetes in your thirties wasn't something either of us saw coming, and I'm so proud of you for how you tackle the challenge of managing it every day. Your dedication to a healthful lifestyle was a major inspiration in putting this cookbook together, and I'm grateful for all of the ways you take care of yourself and me, too. I hope these recipes help to keep our family in good health for many decades to come!

To my friends and family who helped to test recipes for this book (especially my parents, Cindy and Larry Harris, and my friend Lizzie Paulsen), thank you so much for your dedication and feedback.

To my agent Alison Fargis and the team at Stonesong, you are the absolute best! Thank you for all you do to make my cookbook writing career a reality.

To everyone at Ten Speed Press who has been involved in this project, I thank my lucky stars to be able to work with you all and to have your talents go toward creating such gorgeous cookbooks with my name on the cover. It really is a dream. Special thanks to executive editor Lisa Westmoreland, director of marketing Windy Dorresteyn, executive publicist Kristin Casemore, project editor Leigh Saffold, copy editor Sharon Silva, editorial assistant Want Chyi, deputy creative director Emma Campion, designer Annie Marino, production manager Dan Myers, food stylist Nathan Carrabba, prop stylist Claire Mack, and photographer Jennifer Davick.

To Robert Wang, Mary Roy, and the rest of the team at Instant Pot, thank you for authorizing and endorsing my cookbooks for your genius appliance. Since I started my Instant Pot Recipes Facebook page, it's gone from cult favorite to mainstream must-have (I never have to explain what an Instant Pot is anymore!). I'm so glad to be on this adventure with you.

About the Author

Coco Morante is the author of the bestselling *The Essential Instant Pot Cookbook, The Ultimate Instant Pot Cookbook, The Essential Vegan Instant Pot Cookbook,* and *The Ultimate Instant Pot Healthy Cookbook*. She is a recipe developer, facilitator of the Instant Pot Recipes Facebook page, and creator of the blog *Lefty Spoon*. Her recipes and writing have been featured in numerous print and online publications, including *People*, Epicurious, Food Republic, POPSUGAR, TASTE, Kitchn, Simply Recipes, and *Edible Silicon Valley*.

Coco lives in Portland, Oregon, with her husband, Brendan, and their beagle, Beagle Brendan.

Index

T

V

W

Y

Z

Published in the United States by Ten Speed Press, an imprint of Random House, a division of Penguin Random House LLC, New York.
www.tenspeed.com

Library of Congress Cataloging-in-Publication Data

Names: Morante, Coco, author.
Title: The essential diabetes Instant Pot cookbook: healthy, foolproof recipes for your electric pressure cooker / Coco Morante.
Description: Emeryville: Ten Speed Press, 2020. | Includes bibliographical references and index.
Identifiers: LCCN 2019034348 | ISBN 9781984857101 (hardcover) | ISBN 9781984857118 (epub)
Subjects: LCSH: Diabetes--Diet therapy--Recipes. | Smart cookers. | LCGFT: Cookbooks.
Classification: LCC RC662 .M68 2020 | DDC 641.5/6314--dc23
LC record available at https://lccn.loc.gov/2019034348

Hardcover ISBN: 978-1-9848-5710-1
eBook ISBN: 978-1-9848-5711-8

Printed in the United States of America

Design by Annie Marino
Food styling by Nathan Carrabba
Prop styling by Claire Mack

10 9 8 7 6 5 4 3 2 1

First Edition